The Gift of Leadership

The Gift of Leadership

According to the Scriptures

Steven Croft

CANTERBURY
PRESS
Norwich

First published in 2016 by the Canterbury Press Norwich
Editorial office
3rd Floor, Invicta House
108–114 Golden Lane
London EC1Y OTG, UK

Canterbury Press is an imprint of Hymns Ancient & Modern Ltd
(a registered charity)
13A Hellesdon Park Road, Norwich,
Norfolk NR6 5DR, UK

www.canterburypress.co.uk

British Library Cataloguing in Publication data

A catalogue record for this book is available
from the British Library

978 1 84825 865 5

Typeset by Manila Typesetting Company
Printed and bound in Great Britain by
CPI Group (UK) Ltd, Croydon

Contents

Introduction

Leadership according to the Scriptures

Extraordinary influence

Christian people are called to a wide variety of different leadership positions. If you look around an 'ordinary' congregation gathered on a Sunday or during the week, you will find a group of people who exercise extraordinary influence in a wide range of places. This man over here is a police sergeant, responsible for policing a troubled part of the city. This woman in her fifties is a magistrate. The person three rows from the front co-ordinates a local food bank. The person handing out the hymn books today is a secondary-school teacher and head of department. The person getting ready for Sunday School is a grandmother of six. The man serving at the altar has a senior role in a hospital.

This book consists of ten short reflections on passages from the Old Testament on the theme of leadership. They are written for any Christian who is called to exercise influence (which I think is all of us).

The Christian Church today inherits a long tradition of reflection on how to exercise leadership in communities. It stretches back two thousand years to Jesus and more than another thousand years through the Hebrew Bible, the Christian Old Testament, to Moses and to Abraham. This means, I think, that we inherit the longest continuous tradition of reflection on leadership in communities that the human culture has ever seen. I think of it as a deep mine shaft, sunk into the earth, each part built on the one before it.

This mine is full of good things and is not only, or even mainly, for the clergy, those called to exercise leadership in the life of the Church. It is a resource for every Christian who wants to be a better leader: headteachers, health-service managers, shift supervisors, civil servants, entrepreneurs and everyone else.

The mine is not always easy to explore, so think of this short book as a kind of guide book. It's not meant to be an exhaustive study of leadership in the Bible. I've chosen passages and themes which have interested me and which I believe have something to say to leadership in present times.

A personal journey

I've had a lifelong interest in leadership. At the age of 29 I became Vicar of Ovenden, a large parish on the edge of Halifax and the place where my father grew up and where my grandmother still lived. My first year as a vicar felt like putting on a jacket which was several sizes too big. I had to grow into the role.

I had received seven years of full-time education (four at university and three at theological college) followed by almost four years as a curate. I was therefore very surprised to discover that the thing I said to myself over and over again in that first year of leadership was: 'No-one ever taught me how to do this.' Over the years I have pondered exactly what I meant. I did have some idea how to prepare a service or a sermon; how to visit someone in hospital; how to undertake many of the separate tasks which make up the working life of a vicar. But what no-one had taught me was the art of leading a community, a group of people called together to a shared life and to a common goal. I knew almost nothing about how to begin to win trust, to shape a common vision, to enable others in ministry. I knew very little about how difficult and costly leading in communities can be.

That was the start of my journey of learning about leadership. I am still learning. I remained vicar of that parish for over nine years, then for eight years was Warden of Cranmer Hall in Durham, overseeing a community of around 90 men and women preparing for ordained ministry. A different kind of leadership was needed. In 2004, I was invited to set up and lead Fresh Expressions, a national initiative to encourage new forms of Church across the Church of England and the Methodist Church. This new task meant building a team and an organization from scratch, listening to those at the very edge of the church and developing patterns of ministry and training for these new communities. In 2009, I became Bishop of Sheffield, learning to exercise a very different kind of leadership both inside the Church and beyond it in South and East Yorkshire. As this book is published, I am beginning a new ministry as Bishop of Oxford in a very different context and looking forward to fresh challenges in the coming years.

In all of this learning on leadership, I have, of course, learned a great deal from writers and practitioners outside the Church: from the social sciences, from popular literature, from business schools. But I hope I have learned even more from the great tradition of the Church: from the lives of those who have gone before me; from the great writers on leadership and ministry. These include Gregory the Great, Benedict, Augustine and many others. These men and women from the past and the present have all, like me, reflected on the Scriptures, on the great stories passed on to us in the Bible, about those who succeeded and those who failed in their leadership. It is these texts and stories which are the focus of this book.

Finding the help to lead

In all of my study and reflection (and in my experience), one lesson above all stands out. It is that the exercise of leadership in communities is demanding and difficult – far more difficult than it seems. Help is needed.

I know that is true of the ministry of a priest or a bishop, both from my own experience and from conversation with many others. However, I also know it to be true of the experience of those who exercise leadership as politicians, as senior managers, as bankers, as youth leaders. This starting point, that leadership is demanding and difficult, is one of the key insights of the Christian tradition.

Much contemporary literature begins from the opposite position: leadership is basically very simple and straightforward, as long as you buy a particular book, enrol on a particular course or follow a certain set of disciplines. Some teaching on leadership relies on distilling everything down to a few simple lessons which, if mastered, will result in instant success.

But the reality is not like this. The world is a demanding and complex place. We are imperfect people ourselves and we work with imperfect people all the time. Events keep on happening. Resources are scarce. The trajectory of leadership is seldom smooth or simple.

Four domains of leadership

There is no simple way to describe leadership which does justice to the whole Christian tradition. However, for over 12 years now, I have worked with a simple model in the development of my own leadership and in working with and teaching others. It is to describe leadership in four domains:

1 Watching over myself.
2 Working with individuals and teams.
3 Guiding and guarding a community.
4 Leadership in the wider world.

One way of describing these four domains is as a diagram like this:

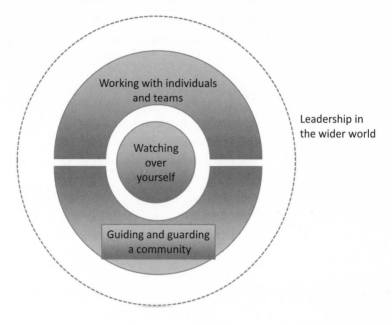

Watching over myself is at the heart of the Christian tradition of leadership: ensuring that the leadership I offer has integrity and balance. The leadership I bring and the influence I offer is put into effect in my leadership of individuals and teams and of the organization or community I am called to serve. Always in my leadership I am called to look beyond that organization to the wider world God has made and to God's purposes within the world.

It may help to have these four domains and this diagram in mind when engaging with the chapters which follow. Some are primarily about one of these four domains, some about the relationship between the four.

For the past twelve years, and through three transitions of role, my reflections on leadership in my own journal and conversations have focused on these four areas and the relationships between them. The model has been tried and tested in personal experience and I don't hesitate to commend it.

Reflections on leadership

My first intention was to write a book of reflections on leadership in the Church, arising from sermons and addresses I have given over the last seven years as Bishop of Sheffield. However, the book became very quickly a series of reflections for Christian leaders in every walk of life (not excluding those involved in church leadership). Over the past couple of years, I have been asked to speak more and more about leadership in a wide range of contexts: to headteachers, business leaders, in a university, to leaders of different faiths. In work I have been asked to lead for the Church of England, I have become more and more convinced of the need for the Church to equip and sustain lay leaders in every walk of life.

The book remains, however, a series of reflections on biblical passages and themes: passages which were given, written down and passed on largely because of what they have to say about leadership in communities by a whole range of people (not simply those called to 'religious' leadership). The Bible contains a wealth of material for such reflection. My choice of passages is a subjective one: these are texts I have returned to again and again over the years for my own reflection on the leadership I offer and in teaching others.

I hope that this book can be read by leaders in a wide range of roles. You will gain most from reading it if you engage yourself with the biblical passage as well as with the reflection. I hope the material will be helpful for small groups to study as well as for individuals. Quotations from the Bible are from the New Revised Standard Version (NRSV) unless otherwise indicated.

I would like to express my thanks to all those who have taught me the lessons of leadership over the years through their lives and through their writing. I have much still to learn.

Steven Croft
March 2016

I

Beginning

1 Kings 12.1–19

*Rehoboam went to Shechem, for all Israel had
come to Shechem to make him king.*

(12.1)

Leadership as service

Shechem may seem a strange place to begin this meditation on
Christian leadership. We've come here because of the story of
Rehoboam, son of Solomon. This is the most powerful story in
the Bible of how not to begin a new leadership responsibility.

Any life offered to God is punctuated by new beginnings. God
calls disciples to new places and new roles. Often these involve
leadership. These moments of change are full of potential and
also full of risk for the leader and for the community. Much
will depend on the way in which a person called into leadership
approaches these times of transition. A good beginning can lead
to learning and transformation for the whole community. But a
bad start can mean disaster.

Rehoboam's name means 'expansion of the people'. It's a
name full of irony in view of what happens here. He became
king over 900 years before Christ, at the height of Israel's power
and influence as a nation. His grandfather, David, battled all his
life to establish a kingdom for the 12 tribes of Israel. His father,
Solomon, consolidated David's reign, built the temple, established the great institutions of Israel and fostered a flourishing
Hebrew culture. David and Solomon each reigned for 40 years.

The Bible makes it clear that in the latter half of Solomon's reign all was not well. But how was Rehoboam to make his new beginning? How was he to handle the legacy of his father and grandfather?

The crown prince gets some things right. First, he pays careful attention to place, to story and to ritual, to the deepest traditions of the nation. Rehoboam calls all the people together in special assembly. He holds the gathering at Shechem: the place where Abram built his first altar to the Lord (Genesis 12.6); the place where Joshua renewed the covenant (Joshua 24); the place where Joseph's bones were buried (Joshua 24.32). This place reminds God's people of their origins, of God's covenant and call, of the great figures of the past.

Second, Rehoboam begins his reign by listening to the people and especially by listening to what is wrong in the life of the nation. Outwardly the nation is secure but on the inside there is decay. Repair and renewal are urgently needed. Transition is a key moment to listen to the voices of dissent and to pay attention to the work of rebuilding. A new leader needs to listen well and see clearly. The situation in Israel could have been saved. This is what the people say:

> Your father made our yoke heavy. Now therefore lighten the hard service of your father and his heavy yoke that he placed on us, and we will serve you. (12.4)

So far so good. Third, Rehoboam asks for time to consider and in that time he takes advice. This is, once again, a good thing. It is a mark of maturity to know that you need help to understand a situation and to know how to respond to it.

Before we move on to think about Rehoboam's mistake, pause a moment to reflect on the three things he got right. He paid attention to the history and story of this community and, by implication, to the founding vision of what the nation was called to be. He paid attention to what people said was wrong in the nation at that moment in its life: he looked and listened. He knew he did not have all the answers and he sought advice and sought that advice from different groups of people.

One of the key tasks of leadership is to offer vision for the future. People called to leadership often wonder where to find fresh vision for the future of a church, a school, a charity, a business, a city or country. There is no deeper challenge.

Vision emerges as leaders do exactly what Rehoboam did in moments of transition. First, reflect on the founding values and vision of a community in its traditions, history and ideals. Take people back to where it began, to the roots, and explore them together. Second, reflect on where that community is now and especially on what is not working. Third, reflect on this gap between the ideal and the reality in many different conversations. As we do these three things, fresh vision for the future begins to emerge exactly in the gap between the ideals of the community and the reality. Rehoboam's story could have been such a strong and powerful beginning.

But that was not to be. Rehoboam seeks his advice in two contrasting places. He takes counsel first with the older men, those who had advised his father, Solomon: 'How do you advise me to answer this people?' (12.9). These older men, with nothing to prove, capture the essence of leadership and new beginnings in their answer:

> If you will be a servant to this people today and serve them and speak good words to them when you answer them, then they will be your servants for ever. (12.7)

Anyone called to a new leadership responsibility would do well to take these words and write them on a card. Pin them to your desk, to your computer, to the inside of the office door, to the reading desk of the pulpit, to the inside cover of your iPad: anywhere where you will see them regularly and be reminded of what they mean. The heart of Christian leadership is to be a servant. The word 'minister' means servant. If you are a Christian and a leader, your calling is primarily to serve and to speak good words to all the people. Power must be mediated through gentleness and humility if communities are not to fracture. Offering leadership as a servant wins trust, confidence and affection. Offering leadership as a servant translates positional power into the kind of authority which can effect change.

When I became Bishop of Sheffield, I held open meetings in every part of the diocese so that we could begin the process of getting to know one another. At each meeting, I gave a short talk and then the floor was open for questions. These were very wide-ranging and stretching. People didn't hold back.

I realized part way through the second meeting what was happening. This was my extended interview for the role. I was being put to the test. I'd already been appointed and installed as Bishop. What was at stake wasn't whether I would continue in the role. What was at stake was whether or not people would take any notice, whether I could win trust, whether the positional leadership of my office could be translated into the kind of authority which can effect change. Most leadership roles bring with them this kind of Shechem moment: the moment of testing and discernment – are we able to trust this person to lead our community forward? Every new beginning will have its time of trial. Those are the moments to remember humility.

Rehoboam then turns to the young men, the ones who have grown up with him and now attend him. They are his contemporaries, his courtiers. They are full of machismo and bravado. They are unseasoned. They are crude. But perhaps they know what Rehoboam wants to hear. The seeds of the nation's destruction have been sown long ago in the neglect of wisdom in the next generation.

Thus shall you say to this people who spoke to you, "Your father made our yoke heavy but you must lighten it for us"; thus shall you say to them, "My little finger is thicker than

my father's loins. Now whereas my father laid on you a heavy
yoke, I will add to your yoke. My father disciplined you with
whips but I will discipline you with scorpions." (12.10)

The story leaves us in suspense for a few moments. We are
not told at this point which advice Rehoboam will follow. Will
he choose the path of humility, of servant leadership, of win-
ning the trust and hearts of his people? Or will he choose the
path of pride, of exerting his position and risk division and
alienation?

On the third day Jereboam and all the people return. The
king gives his reply. He speaks to them 'according to the advice
of the young men' (12.14). A plea for mercy is to be answered
with greater harshness. This one window when division could be
avoided is missed. 'The king did not listen to the people' (12.5).
According to the storyteller, this is a moment like the hardening
of Pharaoh's heart in Exodus. Somehow God's purposes are at
work here for good even in the midst of the tragedy which is
Rehoboam's reign.

But we need to be clear that what we are seeing here is a
tragedy. Rehoboam sows the wind and reaps the whirlwind.
Five sixths of his kingdom is torn away. Civil war will plague
succeeding generations. Political division will lead to religious
apostasy. The people of Israel will worship golden calves again
in the new centres of worship in Bethel and Dan. The fabric of
the nation is immeasurably weakened. Two hundred years later,
the Assyrians will destroy Jereboam's northern kingdom and
its capital, Samaria, in 722 BC. In 587, Jerusalem itself will be
destroyed and Solomon's Temple with it. There will never again
be a strong, united kingdom of Israel, though the dream is one
which will animate prophets and poets for generations still to
come. That dream will lead eventually to the vision of the king
who will come as the true servant to his people, the one who will
be gentle and humble of heart, who will give his very life, who
will establish the reign of God for all time.

A rare wisdom

Sometimes people talk as though leadership in communities and organizations is easy, as though it can be reduced to hints and tips or five points all beginning with the same letter. Lessons about leadership are made to sound simple. That is not a Christian view. True leadership is difficult and complex. The exercise of leadership will stretch us and test us to the limits of what we can bear.

The Bible and the Christian tradition together form the longest continuous reflection on leadership in communities there has ever been. For well over three thousand years, those called to ministry and leadership have reflected in dialogue on the same texts and stories, and have written new ones as a way of passing on wisdom in leadership from one generation to another. One of the absolutely key insights of this whole long tradition until very recently is that leadership in communities is demanding and difficult.[1] There is little that is easy about the exercise of leadership in communities whether you are called to lead in a church, a school, a local authority, a small business or a multinational corporation.

According to the beautiful poem preserved in Job 28, wisdom for leadership is more precious and rare than gold, silver or precious stones that have to be mined from deep in the earth. Gaining that wisdom takes the same effort and engagement. You have to dig deep. It begins with a fear of God and knowledge of yourself before God: in other words, with humility. According to the writings of the Church fathers in the first 600 years of the faith, leadership within the Christian community is more demanding even than leadership in the armed forces, in the medical community or in the government because of the integrity

---

1 For an introduction to this tradition see Christopher A. Beeley, *Leading God's People: Wisdom from the Patristic Tradition for today*, Grand Rapids, MI: Eerdmans, 2012.

required and because of the demanding calling of seeing imperfect people transformed into the likeness and image of God.

All the more reason then to pay very careful attention to the first months of leadership in a new community. Transition is a complex, vulnerable time for the person called to leadership and to the organization they lead. You may find that you have left behind a role in which you were comfortable, and colleagues you loved dearly. You may have come to a strange new place and a job which feels like you are wearing a jacket several sizes too large. You may find that this coincides with moving physically (with your family) to a new place. God has much to teach us in these moments of transition and change but they can be hard. Be sure to take time and space to watch over yourself and those you love in those key months of change as you become re-orientated in a new life and a new role.

For many people, our own insecurity leads directly to a desire to assert ourselves quickly, to somehow prove we are up to the new task. That way lies disaster. A better way in these times of testing is to dive deep into the love of God to find your identity in God's call and God's love and to acknowledge the impossibility of the task in terms of the human resources we bring. There is real joy, I have found, in acknowledging the impossible mission we have been given and a huge relief in saying (if only to ourselves and God), I don't believe I can do this.

The lay theologian Stanley Hauerwas describes in his memoir, *Hannah's Child*, a painful moment when a new Methodist minister was sent to his local congregation. It is a transition that does not go well:

> . . . we were sent a young person to be our pastor who was as ambitious as she was misdirected. In college she had majored in drama. She applied her theatrical skills in her sermons which only made them harder to bear . . . She had been to a church-growth seminar. She told us she knew how to make

the church grow. First, we needed two services . . . Second we would have a phone-a-thon. Finally we would need to learn that we had been far too close-knit as a church.[2]

The pain caused by pride in transitions is immense. Reheboam's errors are still repeated over and over again in churches, schools and businesses. Christians are not immune from uncertain and misguided beginnings. Quarry the deep wisdom and humility from the mine of scripture for every new beginnings you will make in your leadership. Choose to be a servant to the people and serve them and speak good words to them at the beginning of your new responsibility. To do this is to follow the pattern and example of Christ who was himself a servant.

On 13 March 2013, while the world watched, Jorge Mario Bergoglio was elected Pope under his chosen name of Francis. The new Pope immediately gave the Church and the world a powerful lesson in leadership and humility. He refused the more elaborate papal garments. His first request was to ask the assembled crowds to pray for him. He rode back to the same lodgings on the bus with the other cardinals. He refused to move into the elaborate papal apartments. He chose, deliberately and publicly, the path of a servant, the path of humility. He set the tone for all that would follow.

If you and I would aspire to be Christian leaders, we must choose the same path and make the same new beginning. For this is the way of Christ. This is the way trust grows and authority can be exercised in communities all over the world:

If you will be a servant to this people today and serve them and speak good words to them when you answer them, then they will be your servants for ever. (12.7)

---

2 Stanley Hauerwas, *Hannah's Child: A theologian's memoir*, Norwich: SCM Press, 2010, p. 258.

Tending

Psalm 23

Psalm 23 is one of the best known of the psalms. The words give enormous comfort and hope in many different situations. But few people realize today that this psalm is a text about leadership. It holds vital lessons for anyone with the responsibility of leading any kind of organization or community or family. The psalm is a special song of trust and confidence: a kind of creed or statement of faith. Read the familiar words slowly through this lens:

> The LORD is my shepherd, I shall not want.
> He makes me lie down in green pastures;
> he leads me beside still waters;
> he restores my soul.
> He leads me in right paths
> for his name's sake.
>
> Even though I walk through the darkest valley,
> I fear no evil;
> for you are with me;
> your rod and your staff –
> they comfort me.
>
> You prepare a table before me
> in the presence of my enemies;
> you anoint my head with oil;
> my cup overflows.

Surely goodness and mercy shall follow me
all the days of my life,
and I shall dwell in the house of the LORD
my whole life long.

A shepherd of the people

The image of the shepherd in the psalms is first and foremost an image of leadership. The psalm is the prayer of a leader, a servant of God's people, expressing trust in the Lord who leads and guides.

Many of the psalms collected in the Bible were originally used in public worship in the temple. The king, the leader of the nation, played an active role in that worship. In some of the psalms, the congregation pray for God's blessing on the king (20, 21 and 72). Some psalms tell of the special relationship between God and the king (2 and 110). Some psalms are written to be sung by the king in the worship (or by a solo singer acting the king's part in the ritual). These psalms describe the trials and experiences of the king as he leads the nations (18 and 118).

Psalm 23 is best read as this kind of psalm: a psalm to be prayed in worship by the king. There are two main clues to this reading. The first is that the psalmist is in a special relationship with God and has been anointed (v. 5). Kings were anointed at their coronation. The Hebrew word for anointed one is 'Messiah' and the Greek word for anointed is 'Christ'. The second is the use of the term 'my shepherd' in the opening line.

The term 'shepherd' was a common image for the leader of the nation throughout the ancient world. This common image of leadership is lost on us today. We no longer describe our Prime Minister or monarch as a shepherd. But the picture is common throughout the Old Testament and across the ancient Near East (see, for example, Numbers 27.17, 1 Kings 22.17,

Ezekiel 34.2–6). When God is described as shepherd of the nation (as in Psalm 95 or 78), this, too, is a picture of God's reign, God's leadership and God's kingship.

Psalm 23 is, therefore, first and foremost a reflection on leadership. The king is the shepherd of the people. Now this shepherd of God's people declares that the Lord, the God of Israel, is his own shepherd. In the midst of the temple, on a day of great pilgrimage and festival, as the nation gathers in solemn assembly, no matter what the troubles of the past year, the king sings of the goodness and faithfulness of God. He places himself once again under the reign and authority of God. His own leadership comes from God, to whom he must give account.

In the New Testament this image is expanded and developed still further. Jesus describes himself as the Good Shepherd in John 10.11–18.

> 'I am the good shepherd. The good shepherd lays down his life for the sheep.' (10.11)

Jesus identifies himself here with God's kingship (in the phrase 'I am') and also as the anointed one who will come to reign. Service and sacrifice and a mission to the whole world are at the heart of Jesus' understanding of leadership:

> 'I have other sheep that do not belong to this fold. I must bring them also and they will listen to my voice. So there will be one flock, one shepherd.' (10.16)

It is not hard to see why this image of the shepherd is also used in the New Testament to describe the leadership and ministry in the life of the Church. Jesus' commission to Peter is to 'feed my lambs . . . tend my sheep . . . feed my sheep' (John 21.15–17). Paul's words in Acts 19 to the elders at Miletus are echoed and referenced in every ordination service:

'Keep watch over yourselves and over all the flock of which the Holy Spirit has made you overseers, to shepherd the church of God that he obtained with the blood of his own Son.' (Acts 20.28–29)

In a similar way, 1 Peter uses the image of the shepherd to describe the task of leading God's people:

. . . tend the flock of God that is in your charge, exercising the oversight, not under compulsion but willingly, as God would have you do it, not for sordid gain but eagerly. Do not lord it over those in your charge but be examples to the flock. And when the chief shepherd appears, you will win the crown of glory that never fades away. (1 Peter 5.2–4)

Those called to lead in the life of the Church will always need to pay careful attention to the call to be a shepherd. It is for this reason that a Bishop's pastoral staff is in the form of a shepherd's crook. But this call to tend, to be a shepherd, has much to say as well to Christians who exercise leadership beyond the church, in hospitals, business, schools, government and industry. The earliest and broadest use of the term, in Psalm 23, is in the leadership of the nation not simply the care of the church. All Christian leaders are called to lead as God leads.

Pride and Anxiety

Here are two reflections from this ancient text about leading well. The first and the simplest is that good leadership springs from a healthy relationship with God. I am able to be a good shepherd only because I am able to say: 'The LORD is my shepherd.'

All authority in heaven and on earth belongs to God. The only basis on which I am able to exercise authority and leadership is by acknowledging this fundamental truth. Any leadership I offer, in the Church or the world, flows from God's leadership and needs to be exercised within a framework of accountability to God and to others.

As the people of Israel recognized in their worship, this is what makes leadership safe. Sadly, it is not difficult to think of the dangers of bad, unaccountable leadership in national or local government, in schools, churches or businesses. The exercise of authority and power is very demanding: potentially life giving but potentially dangerous. For that reason there needs to be a clear framework of human accountability to people and structures but also, ultimately, accountability to God.

But this is not only about safeguarding. It is also about the inner confidence and identity to lead well. This too comes ultimately from a relationship with God. All traditions about leadership understand that knowing yourself is key to the exercise of good leadership. A fundamental part of knowing yourself, for a Christian, rests in knowing you are loved by God, deeply, personally, powerfully. The leadership we offer should flow from being rooted in the love and care of God and in God's call.

Many people who are called to leadership grapple with questions of pride. We quickly become full of ourselves and our own importance and our leadership suffers in consequence. The Bible and other stories down the ages are full of tales of human pride leading to a fall. The antidote to this poison is rooting our leadership in humility before God and others. To say 'the LORD is my shepherd' is to gain that wisdom and perspective which are vital to the task. Without it we will become puffed up with our own self-importance and ultimately we will fail as leaders.

But even more people called to leadership grapple with the opposite dilemma: low confidence, anxiety, fear and self-doubt. Our leadership is fearful. We lack the confidence either to take on a leadership position or truly to lead when we find ourselves in a position of responsibility and influence. The headteacher hides in her office rather than confront the discipline problems in the playground. The vicar ignores and avoids the bully on the Church council. The shift supervisor overlooks the pilfering going on under his nose for fear of provoking a confrontation. The nurse manager longs to improve the systems but dares not take the first step. Our leadership is less than it could be.

Where do Christian leaders find the courage and confidence to overcome self-doubt and fear and fulfil the responsibilities of our office? Almost always, real leadership will involve taking the difficult, not the easy, road. In the words of 1 John, perfect love casts out fear (1 John 4.18). Courage comes from time spent reflecting on God's love, through declaring at the beginning of each day and in the midst of each crisis: 'The LORD is my shepherd, I shall not want.'

Psalm 23 reminds us that we are held in the great, unsearchable, personal love of God. The words need to shape our working lives. They remind us that God in his great love will provide; that in the midst of the demands of leadership there will be green pastures and still waters, rest and re-creation. In all the complexity of our decision making, God will guide us and lead us. In the midst of suffering and difficulty and our care of others, even in the midst of great evil, God's love abides. There is nowhere beyond the reach of God's love and nothing in all creation, in life or death, which can separate us from that love revealed in Jesus Christ.

One of the great and subtle temptations of leadership is to neglect the inner life and your relationship with God because of the many things which demand immediate attention. Long ago, one of the wisest of Christian leaders wrote these words:

Often it happens that when a man undertakes the cares of government, his heart is distracted with a diversity of things and, as his mind is divided among many interests and becomes confused, he finds he is unfitted for any of them.[1]

---

1 Gregory the Great, *Pastoral Rule*, 1.4.

Leadership contains its own distractions and temptations and, after pride, the first of these is over-busyness leading to exhaustion. The practice of reflection, of prayer, of being centred in the love of God revealed in Christ, is absolutely essential to good Christian leadership in any organization. The responsibility of personal prayer is as serious for the Christian head of a hospital or college as it is for an archbishop. It is only in prayer and reflection that we find freedom to rest and the resources of courage essential to leadership, which are found in God's grace and love.

That will mean that every Christian leader in any sphere of life will need to pay careful attention to prayer: setting aside the time; learning good disciplines of daily prayer; finding strength, perspective and renewal in worship which feeds and supports your working life; taking time in the rhythm of each week and each year to rest, to withdraw, to retreat and to walk more deeply with the Good Shepherd.

Watching over yourself is fundamental to good leadership (Acts 20.28 again). At the heart of watching over yourself is creating space to nurture your own deep friendship with the living God, to constantly lift up your heart to God's gentle care, finding the deep springs of living water which will sustain you in the demanding task to which God has called you. Look for the paths of grace, the green pastures, the still waters. Learn to lead from a sure and continual knowledge of God's love.

Caring for each other

And so to the second of our two reflections. The king as shepherd of the people prays: 'The LORD is my shepherd.' The implication is clear. As the Lord is a shepherd to us, so in the same way we are to be a shepherd to others. The words of Jesus in John 20.21 are a commission to lead: 'As the Father has sent me, so I send you.'

At the heart of Christian leadership in any organization is the call to tend people, relationships and communities. The word 'tend' is another word for love, of course, carrying the emphasis of gentleness or tenderness.

Every leader in every organization must focus attention on the task in hand, whatever that may be. But wise leaders (and particularly Christian leaders) must also pay attention to tending the people, the relationships, the culture which gives life to that organization. Without such tending, the task will not be done and those involved may find that they are damaged in the process.

For the past six years I have been privileged to sit on the Archbishops' Council, the senior trustee body of the Church of England. We meet for whole days or for residentials and more or less the whole national life of the Church of England passes through our meetings. Necessarily, it is a group of strong leaders with a large and complex task.

The Archbishops' Council has a work consultant, a person of remarkable wisdom, who sits in on our meetings, observes them all and offers her reflections at the end. The word Gillian uses most in her reflections is 'tend'. Over and over again she encourages us to tend and attend to our relationships within the group and with others, to the trust between us so that we will be able to do the task for which we have come together.

So many organizations (and, alas, some churches) focus on the tasks only and not on this tending, this gentle attention to relationships which enables the tasks to be done.

Psalm 23 unpacks what it means to tend, to shepherd, those whom we are called to lead. It will involve, among other things, setting a pace which is realistic and an organizational culture in which people can grow and thrive. Every organization needs its equivalent of green pastures and still waters. Every leader will find the need to make people lie down from time to time. Are we building a culture and an organization in which people are able to grow and thrive over the long term? Can the pace be sustained? Are there quieter times in the week and in the year? Can those we work with find rest for their souls? Is this community sustainable?

To tend means to pay particular attention to individuals and communities in times of great suffering and difficulty. These times come in every life and in every community. Christian leaders have a particular responsibility to be present, to be there in those moments.

In the period when I was responsible for a college training men and women for ministry, three of our students died in the space of six months. One was a young woman in her early twenties who collapsed and died in the college fitness room. The whole college was caught up in grief in her death, in hosting her family when they came to Durham, in sending representatives to her funeral, in remembering her. My responsibility as a leader in that community was primarily to tend to those who were grieving for a time, not to recall us to the task. Productivity fell in terms of teaching and learning. We walked together through the valley of the shadow of death. For all the sorrow, the college community was marked by a particular tenderness in that year which I have never forgotten.

To tend means also to celebrate and nurture through meals and hospitality. The deepest conversations in human life happen around tables. Ann and I have been blessed with four children, now in their twenties and thirties. Like many other parents, we have discovered that there is vital furniture you need more than any other if you are going to create a healthy family or any kind of healthy community and organization: a table and chairs. It is no accident that most parish churches set a table and a meal at the heart of all that they do.

Community is created as we eat together. Hospitality is a key means of tending and extending loving care. Growing good relationships through hospitality will be at the heart of all Christian leadership.

The right kind of confidence

The wrong kind of confidence in leadership can lead to disaster: confidence in your own self and abilities, confidence based only around objectives and not around the flourishing of the people who make up every organization.

The right kind of confidence is life giving. This is confidence rooted in relationship with the living, loving God. This is confidence that takes seriously God's care for you as leader (and therefore takes seriously the call to watch over yourself). This is confidence that takes seriously the call to tend people and relationships, to enable human flourishing, to balance task with a desire to see people grown, through healthy patterns of work and rest, in times of suffering and distress, through grace and hospitality and friendship. This is the kind of confidence that comes through being able to say, all down the years of our leadership, 'The LORD is my shepherd.'

3

Hope

Ezekiel 47.1–12

Everything will live where the river goes.

(47.9)

Look to the future

Christian leaders are called to be people of hope, wherever we may lead. Hope is rare in the world and always has been. Hope is the capacity to see a different and more positive future in any context and find the energy to begin to change things. Hope is what is needed in a failing school, an empty and divided church, a fractious board room, a demoralized social services department, a refugee camp, an ineffective GP practice, an unprofitable business, a charity which has lost its way. A mere sliver of hope makes a difference.

The most remarkable study of hope in the Bible stands as part of the legacy of a prophet called Ezekiel. Ezekiel was born and lived in Jerusalem over 600 years before Christ. He was part of the first generation of exiles taken to live in Babylon in 597 BC. Part of Ezekiel's calling is to be a prophet of reality. His task is to help the exiles and the people left in Jerusalem understand that the destruction of Jerusalem is somehow the judgement of God on the nation. But the other part of his calling is to be a prophet of hope, casting a vision of new life, restoration and renewal.

Our passage is part of the long, final series of visions for the future which begins in 40.1–2:

In the twenty-fifth year of our exile, at the beginning of the year, in the fourteenth year after the city was struck down.

This prophet has lived through the invasion of his homeland, the exile of his people, the destruction of his city, the demolition of his temple and the end of his nation. For 25 years he has lived in exile. He has stared desolation in the face and contemplated the grace and wonder of Almighty God. What does he see?

The river

Then he brought me back to the entrance of the temple; there water was flowing from below the threshold of the temple . . . (47.1)

Ezekiel has described a new temple in the midst of the desert. And now, at the end of his vision, he sees a tiny trickle of water, like a teardrop, flowing from the altar, the place of prayer and sacrifice. This tiny stream emerges from the threshold, the edge, the place of liminal encounter.

The stream which flows is at first a trickle, like a raindrop down a window. You wouldn't notice it. Ezekiel and his guide measure a thousand cubits as they follow the tiny stream – about a 20-minute walk. This tiny trickle of water is now ankle deep. They walk on for a further thousand cubits. They are walking, of course, through a dry and dusty wilderness where nothing grew. The water is now knee deep. Another thousand cubits. Ezekiel's guide leads him into and through the water and it is waist deep.

Again he measured one thousand cubits and it was a river that I could not cross, for the water had risen. It was deep enough to swim in, a river that could not be crossed. (47.5)

Ezekiel has now walked just over a mile from the threshold of the temple. The rising flow of the river is only part of the miracle. The prophet and his guide now retrace their steps to the temple. On either side of the river, there is abundant life. The soil is very fertile, full of seeds. Where this river flows, everything lives. There are trees of every kind. They bear fresh fruit not every year but every month, good to eat, like the trees in the Garden of Eden. Such is the life-giving power of the river that the leaves on these trees do not wither, nor does their fruit fail. There is no autumn or winter in this land. Their leaves are for healing. These wonderful trees are a source of abundant life and wholeness of life.

All this Ezekiel sees in his vision. But his guide tells him (and us) even more about the river of life. This river flows into the landlocked sea south of Jerusalem known the world over as the Dead Sea.

The Dead Sea is 1,400 feet below sea level, earth's lowest elevation on land. It is almost 1,000 feet deep, 30 miles long and nine miles wide. The Jordan river and several other streams flow into it. Nothing flows out. It is ten times as salty as the ocean. The Dead Sea is called the Dead Sea for a simple reason. It is completely dead. Nothing lives in that vast expanse of water. There are no fish. There are no aquatic plants. Minuscule quantities of bacteria and fungi are present. But the world over, the Dead Sea is the archetypal symbol of the place where nothing lives. It is the one place on the planet where there are no plants or animals.

Ponder this carefully. It is wonderful to bring life to the desert and that is miracle enough. But the Dead Sea is something else entirely.

What happens when this tiny trickle of water, this teardrop from the place of prayer and sacrifice has grown into a stream and then into a river and enters the sea, the sea of stagnant water. We are told 'the water will become fresh.' Such is the power of this flow.

Wherever the river goes everything will live. People will stand fishing beside the sea from En-gedi to En-eglaim (two settlements on the shore). It will be a place for the spreading of nets. Its fish will be of a great many kinds, like the fish of the Great Sea . . . (47.8–10)

Everything will live where the River goes. The desert has become the Garden of Eden. The Dead Sea is filled with life. We miss the size and scope of God's promises. Everything will live where the River goes.

Keeping faith

God gave to Ezekiel a whole series of extraordinary visions of hope the like of which the world has never seen. A valley of dry bones is reassembled and becomes a mighty army. People with hearts of stone are given hearts of flesh. God comes as the true Shepherd to look for his people. A barren desert is turned into a fruitful garden. The Dead Sea is filled with abundant life.

Christian leaders, whatever their sphere of work, are called to be the successors of Ezekiel: women and men of hope. Women and men who are shown deserts and see visions of beautiful gardens. Women and men who are taken to places where no fish have been caught for many a long year, and see an abundant harvest for the kingdom.

We are called to be women and men of vision and possibility, called to stir up and lead God's people in the midst of their exile, in the midst of the desert and point to the living God who brings life. We are called to be prophets with impossible dreams and visions, agents of change in the church and in the world, held captive by the love of God and speaking words of life to all we meet. We are called to courage, to big visions, to rage against the dying of the light, to lead God's church and God's world in new pathways in all the places where God calls us.

In all of this, we are called to cherish hope and grow in hope. This is not an easy task in a doubting and sceptical world and a Church which is more given to despair than vision. The world around us believes that hope is merely a mood: a set of cheery emotions which visit us in spring or on sunny bank holidays or after a glass or two of wine.

But in Christian theology, hope is not a mood. Hope is a virtue: strength of character. Remember Paul's words at the end of 1 Corinthians 13.3:

Meanwhile these three remain, faith, hope and love . . .

We understand, still, that love is something we are meant to practise every day, even though we do not feel like it. We cannot love only when the mood takes us. Love must be as constant as the hills. We understand a little that faith is something we are meant to practise every day even though we do not feel like it.

But in our wider culture and in much of the Church, we have lost all sense that hope is something we are meant to practise every day, even in the midst of the desert, of the exile, on the shores of the Dead Sea. We are called to be hopeful every day just as we are called to love every day and believe every day. This Christian hope should be the wellspring of our leadership.

The shape of time

Ezekiel's vision was not born from his optimistic personality on a sunny spring day in Babylon when all was right in the world. Ezekiel's vision is born from 25 long years of cherishing and practising hope, this most slender and powerful of virtues. Hope gave Ezekiel the courage to face the reality of Israel's situation; to dig deep into the tradition, to imagine that things could be different, to hold out impossible visions, to turn people back to the grace of God. His words still inspire us two and a half thousand years after he wrote of water flowing from the threshold of the temple. Where does that sense of hope come from?

Ezekiel's hope is born of God. The journey he is called to make in coming to terms with disaster is a complete stripping back of every ground for hope. It is no longer possible for him to be merely optimistic on the grounds that there are some good people in the nation, or that good luck will return, or that the signs of the times are slightly better. Ezekiel has a vision of God. It is a vision of God's greatness and majesty and holiness and grace. His hope is born in that vision and in keeping that vision of God alive in the midst of his people.

It is not an accident that the tiny stream of new life rises from the altar, the place of worship and sacrifice, the place where we catch week by week and year by year a fresh vision of the living God. Ezekiel's vision holds together worship and the transformation of the whole world from a desert to a fruitful paradise. The energy for change flows from the worship of God's people.

Worship plays a vital role in nurturing hope in Christian leaders. If Ezekiel is to be believed, the most important thing you can do in the week to sustain your leadership in the world is to go to church. It is in the place of worship that we regain our perspective on the nature of God and the place of our work in God's world. It is in the place of worship that we are refreshed and renewed to begin again, Monday by Monday, in the leadership we offer. It is in the place of worship that we catch again that elusive Christian perspective on time which is so hard to maintain in a world which does not acknowledge God's reign.

For a Christian leader, time has a particular shape. It is not an endless cycle with all things returning in their season. It is not a succession of ages with each one worse than the one before so that we look back to a golden past. It is not the story of relentless human progress and evolution towards a perfect future where all problems will be solved.

Time has this shape. God created the heavens and the earth and created humankind and God's creation is good. Humanity is deeply flawed and the flaws in humankind affect the good creation God has made. All is not as God would have it be.

God sent his Son, Jesus, to be the Saviour of the world and to proclaim God's reign. God's kingdom is established in the life and death and resurrection of Jesus Christ. But God's kingdom is not yet here in all its fullness. As Christians we look forward to the day when Christ will come again, when God's reign of peace and justice will be established in the earth.

We are called to live in between the time when Christ established the kingdom and the time when Christ will return in glory. This is the time when the Church prays each day 'Your kingdom come, your will be done on earth as it is in heaven.' This is the time when we are called to live in hope: the hope that Christ will come again at the end of the ages and the hope that change is possible in this present world. Christian leaders are called to be agents of God's change in the world, reshaping the communities we serve and building God's church and kingdom.

Each time we come to worship and especially when we gather in the Eucharist, this deeply Christian and distinctive sense of time is restored and refreshed. We look back in the creed and the Eucharistic prayer to the creation and to the life, ministry, death and resurrection of Jesus Christ. We look within and around us in prayers of confession and intercession, bringing before God the needs of the world, as the Spirit groans within us as we pray. We listen to God's word, reflecting on the meaning of the gospel for our lives and for our world. We look ahead to the time when Christ will return and the Church will feast with him in his kingdom. We seek fresh strength for the ministry and leadership we are called to exercise day by day in our vocation.

Re-kindling hope

In every generation, Christian leaders are called to be people of hope. We struggle to imagine what it must have been like for our parents and grandparents called to rebuild Europe after the devastation of two world wars. We can scarcely understand what it must be like to be a Christian and a leader in Rwanda after genocide or in Syria today.

In the same way, how do you make a beginning as a Christian teacher in your first classroom in a failing inner city school? How do you fulfil your office as a local councillor or trade union official in a community where all hope is gone? How do you make a new beginning as a vicar or pastor in a church which has forgotten how to love?

Christian leaders are called to be men and women of hope, to serve in a wilderness and to rebuild lives and communities.

They will be people who are rooted and grounded in worship and a vision of God sustained by worship. They will be people who understand that new life flows from small, imperceptible beginnings and takes time to grow. They will be people who believe that one person of faith can make a powerful, lasting difference over time. They will be people who believe that where the river flows, everything will live.

4

Pain

1 Kings 19

. . . and after the fire, the sound of sheer silence.

(19.12)

Fear and pain

Leadership is difficult at a number of levels. It is often genuinely difficult to know what to do, where to begin, how to behave, where to set priorities. In those moments, a leader needs to move slowly, listen well, put on humility and be a servant to those we are attempting to lead. To lead well is to be perplexed often.

But there is a second level of difficulty for those who lead: coping somehow with the fear and the pain and the exposure which leadership brings both when things go well and when things do not. If we are not watchful in those moments then our leadership will be undermined or derailed by the inner storms which follow.

Gregory wrote these words in his *Pastoral Rule*. They offer an early description of breakdown in leadership:

And indeed what else is power in the post of superiority but a tempest of the mind wherein the ship of the heart is ever shaken by hurricanes of thought. It is ceaselessly driven to and fro, until, by sudden excesses of words and deeds it founders on confronting rocks.[1]

---

1 Gregory, *Pastoral Rule*, 1.9.

Everyone who exercises leadership will recognize that some things keep all of us awake at night: the difficult decision involving a close colleague; the meeting which took a wrong turn; the angry letter or email; the worry about what people think of us; the concern about how we will deliver that project.

At some points of great stress, those fears and anxieties build, like a storm inside us. If we do not recognize this and take care then, in Gregory's image, the ship of the heart is driven before them and they will burst out in sudden excesses of words and deeds. Leadership (and the lives of leaders and their families) are shipwrecked.

I have several textbooks on leadership on my bookshelf. Some are weighty, academic tomes from business schools. Others are more popular. Hardly any of them have even a single chapter on how to cope with the fear and pain involved in leadership. Except one.

Elijah's journey

The story of the prophet Elijah is told mainly in 1 Kings and the beginning of 2 Kings. Elijah is a prophet of God, called to leadership in the northern kingdom. In his day, he is the leader of the opposition, a difficult role but one found in many different contexts today.

King Ahab is drawing the nation away from the worship of the God of Israel and encouraging the worship of Baal, the fertility cult of Canaan. Behind Ahab stands the menacing figure of Jezebel, his queen from Sidon, who longs for Ahab to be a tyrant like the kings of other nations. The stage is set for a dramatic power struggle.

That struggle reaches its climax in the dramatic encounter between Elijah and the prophets of Baal told in 1 Kings 18. All the people are assembled on Mount Carmel. Elijah invites the prophets of Baal to choose and prepare a bull, to set it on a pile of wood and call on Baal to set the sacrifice alight. Nothing happens.

Elijah then takes his bull, sets it on the wood, pours water over the sacrifice three times and calls on the Lord to set the offering alight. It is a moment of high drama. Fire falls from heaven and consumes the sacrifice. There is a great victory. Rain is restored after three years of drought.

But in the next chapter we discover the pain and the inner cost of Elijah's leadership. Jezebel puts out a contract on Elijah's life. There is physical danger and he flees south. But there is more to his dilemma than this.

It is clear from the verses which follow that Elijah is exhausted and overextended in his leadership and near the end of what he can bear. He is isolated, fearful and questioning the meaning of his life. Elijah is running away from far more than Jezebel's threats: 'It is enough now, LORD, take away my life' (19.4).

How does God respond to Elijah's pain in leadership?

The story is told in two parts. First there is a long journey into the wilderness, a journey back to the beginning. In the way the story is told, the Lord travels with Elijah, watches over him and tends him.

> He looked and there at his head was a cake baked on hot stones and a jar of water. He ate and drank and lay down again. The angel of the LORD came a second time, touched him and said, 'Get up and eat, otherwise the journey will be too much for you.' (19.6–7)

One of the most common experiences of leadership in a whole variety of contexts is this feeling of being overextended, exhausted and misunderstood. It can happen in those moments when we make mistakes. The more public the mistake, the more acute the feelings of stress. There is no leader alive who does not make mistakes. However, it can also happen in those moments when stress accumulates and we are simply over-busy for too long. There is a cost to leadership even when everything is going well. Again, there is no leader alive who is able to live a completely balanced and ordered life. Moments of stress accumulate and, every so often, create a crisis.

As a Christian leader, in those moments, how do you believe God responds to your mistake or your feeling of being stretched and overextended or your exhaustion? How does God respond when you cry out in this pain: 'It is enough, now, LORD'?

It's an important question. Our image of God is sometimes a projection of many experiences and needs to be tested against Scripture. The last thing we need in a moment of genuine pain and difficulty is an image of a God who is a hard task master and does not listen.

In this story, God responds to his servant, Elijah, with the gift of space, of security, of tenderness, of practical provision, of attention, of mercy. In one of the great crises of Elijah's life, this rebuilding is not the work of a moment. Elijah journeys for forty days and forty nights from Beersheba, where he left his servant, to Horeb, the mountain of God, sustained by the food the angel has provided for him. God travels with him, goes before him, ministers to him each step of the way. Part of the healing at least is in this journey, this retreat.

The still, small voice

But rest and safety and a journey in this instance are not enough. The great crisis in the life of the nation has been brought to a head on Mount Carmel. But the consequences of that in Elijah's life have been severe. His whole being reverberates still with the encounter – even though this moment would be seen for years to come as a great victory.

God leads him to Mount Horeb, the place where the law was given to Moses and to the people of Israel, one of the founding places in the life of the nation. In that place, God gives to Elijah his servant the gift of an enduring and extraordinary encounter with lessons for leadership in many spheres and every generation.

Elijah has been strengthened through his journey. He is now able to come face to face with God on the mountain of the Lord: face to face with reality, with truth, with purpose. How does that encounter take place?

Now there was a great wind, so strong that it was splitting mountains and breaking rocks in pieces before the LORD, but the LORD was not in the wind; and after the wind an earthquake, but the LORD was not in the earthquake; and after the earthquake a fire, but the LORD was not in the fire; and after the fire, a sound of sheer silence. (19.11–12)

The final phrase is hard to translate. The 'still, small voice' of the Authorized Version remains my preferred wording.

Elijah needs to be held in the presence of God long enough for the storms raging within him from this great crisis of his life to be worked out. The story externalizes them as the great crashing wind, the earthquake, shaking the foundations of his life, the fire which threatens to consume him. God has taken Elijah away into the wilderness so that this turmoil can be faced honestly and safely. As the stress and turmoil subsides, so the voice of God is heard once more in stillness and in peace.

God's question is unchanged at the end of the encounter and so are Elijah's words to God. But now Elijah is able to hear again God's words to him. In the newfound silence of his heart and mind, it is possible to listen to the God who whispers and find fresh direction. There is a renewal of his vocation: Elijah's purpose now is to pass on the mantle of leadership to the next generation, to raise up others who will follow him. The crisis has passed.

Building resilience

Elijah's experience was at one of the key crisis moments in his life. Most leaders will encounter such moments at some points when a number of different factors come together to increase the demands on us beyond breaking point. Some of my own time as a bishop is spent each year with those who have reached this kind of crisis, trying to walk with them on this part of the journey.

There are certainly lessons to be learned for this kind of life crisis: lessons about rest, withdrawal, support, time away from the role, sabbaticals, journeys and prayer. But the lessons of 1 Kings 19 have a much wider application for the more ordinary moments of our leadership.

Few people, I think, experience leadership as a steady-state equilibrium in which we approach each day and each decision in a similar way. Stuff happens in our leadership which affects us internally and therefore affects the way we behave and the decisions we make. Sometimes we may be hurt or frightened, angry or vulnerable, confused or depressed by the things that happen to us during the day. How do we process all of that?

Every child learns punctuation in primary school. We learn that a page of text needs full stops and paragraphs, commas and semi-colons in order to make sense to others, to be read and to be understood.

Elijah's story also underlines the importance of punctuation, not in the printed text but in a life. Resilience is a key part of the leadership any Christian offers. Resilience is ability to respond well to stress and pressure, to make good decisions within it and still to remain yourself. As we grow in years and responsibility, God's purpose is that we become more resilient not less, able to cope with more and greater responsibility.

But a vital part of learning resilience is learning to punctuate our lives with opportunities for rest, for reflection, for allowing the inner storms to die down, for processing the emotional wash of our own leadership and organizations. How do we do that?

The most fundamental place for processing all the stuff that happens is the place of prayer and reflection. Often when clergy talk to others about learning to pray regularly, it can sound as through we are simply encouraging people to be pious for its own sake.

Finding and building a habit of prayer, for a Christian, is a vital part of the leadership we offer in any sphere. It is in prayer that we find stillness in the midst of the storm, time for the waves to subside, perspective on the day that has passed and the day that is to come and the strength to put on again the Christian virtues of faith, hope and love. It is in prayer that we discern God's hand, find joy afresh, reset our inner compass to true north. Prayer is that vital pause at the beginning and end of the day, the quiet time which makes all the difference in the world to the way that day is lived.

Habits of daily prayer can seem hard to learn. Like all good habits, they are as hard to instil as bad ones are to give up. You will need to give some careful thought to where and how you might form the habit of daily prayer and what will help or hinder you. Finding a friend or a minister to talk this through with often helps (as you would talk to a personal trainer or a doctor about physical fitness). It may seem hard at the beginning of a busy day on the factory floor or on the wards to get up 30 minutes earlier in order to have time to pray. It is well worth it for the time and the space to process the storms and currents of leadership and to listen for the still small voice at the beginning of each day.

For many people, including me, there are two other vital ways of processing the stuff that happens to us as leaders. Different personality types may favour one of these above the other. For me, both have a vital place.

The first is the habit of solitary reflection through writing a journal. Every six weeks or so, I carve out some time to look back at what I have been doing and think about where the time has gone. At the same time I look ahead to the next month or two and reset both my attitude and my objectives. I do all of this through writing a journal: a systematic exercise in reflection. I've been keeping my present journal continuously now for around twelve years and journalling on and off probably for 30 years. I used to journal longhand in an exercise book but my handwriting became so bad, I switched some years ago to a Word document.

Journalling gives me a way to pull complex thoughts, anxieties and puzzles out of my head and set them down on the printed page. Journalling helps me face the reality of what I have been doing, where time has gone, what went well, what went badly, where the learning needs to happen, where priorities need to be reset. It is another form of punctuation and a vital part of any leadership I offer.

The second way of processing and reflection is conversation and review. Some of that conversation and review takes place with close colleagues. But the most valuable conversations are usually outside those working relationships with the people I turn to for work consultancy and spiritual direction. Again, this is a regular, structured time, three or more times per year, surrounded by written reflection, where I have learned to work out through dialogue both some of the stresses of leadership and ministry and some of the more complex decisions I face.

Stillness

This chapter ends with a hymn based around three passages from scripture (Psalm 62.1, Psalm 131.2 and Luke 1.78). It's a poem written in the early morning which tries to capture something of what happens when we wait with God at the beginning of each day, recreating in our own daily lives the experience of Elijah in 1 Kings 19.

On God alone my soul in stillness waits
My scattered heart his mercy recreates
The desolate and grieving celebrate
Wait on God in stillness O my soul
Rest in God in stillness O my soul.

In God alone my soul in silence rests
An anxious child upon its mother's breast
In his mercy all who come are blessed
Hope in God in stillness O my soul
Trust in God in stillness O my soul.

For God alone my soul in darkness longs
My fractured heart forgiven all its wrongs
The dawn awakens tender living songs
Walk with God in stillness O my soul
Rise with God in stillness O my soul.[2]

2 The words are set to the tune 'Cenedius', the tune of the hymn, 'O welcome all ye noble saints of old' (God and man at table are sat down).

5

Team

For the task is too heavy for you; you cannot do it alone.

(18.18)

Evolving leadership

Here is another verse for leaders in all walks of life to memorize, write on a card, place above the lintel of their office and on the inside cover of their iPad. There is a limit to what any single person can do alone. Every good leader will work in and through a team.

If you are leading well, then you will notice that the situation you are responsible for will begin to change and evolve. Some problems will be solved and new challenges will appear. The external environment may change. The organization or your responsibilities within it may begin to grow.

As this begins to happen, the leader will need to take note of two things. The first is that your own role will need to change and evolve. As a vicar, I found that my role continued to evolve with every year that passed. The church I was leading grew from a hundred people to two hundred people to three hundred people. As that change happened I could no longer visit all those who were ill, lead all the services or even know every member of the congregation. I had to give careful thought to what my role was and should be as those changes happened (and, with hindsight, I didn't always get that right or understand it or explain it well).

The second change is that as this particular community grew larger, part of my role was to make sure that the structures and skeleton of community life grew to keep pace with the community. The church needed different ways of building family and community, of welcoming new members, of pastoring and teaching, of belonging and identity.[1]

It's not difficult to find parallels to my experience as a vicar in other forms of leadership. Imagine a skilled primary-school teacher who becomes first a deputy head, then a head of school without classroom responsibility, then an executive head with responsibility for two other schools. Each step demands a change in leadership offered. Each step demands that thought is given to the right team and leadership structures for the school or the group of schools.

Or else imagine two entrepreneurs who leave university and found a small web design company, which also makes computer games. Ten years later, that one small company has grown to become a network of three companies employing over a hundred people and is set for further expansion. How many changes of role have the two co-founders navigated in that time? How many times has the structure of the organization changed to support its own growth?

Doing too much

One of the longest studies of leadership in the Scriptures is the story of Moses, told across the Books of Exodus, Leviticus, Numbers and Deuteronomy. Moses, with Elijah, is one of the great figures of the Old Testament. Like many of the great figures from the Bible, we learn as much, if not more, from Moses' mistakes as from the things he did well. We will return to his story in further reflections in this book.

---

1 I wrote about some of these changes in my book, *Transforming Communities*, London: Darton, Longman and Todd, 2002.

Consider for a moment how Moses' leadership role changed through the whole course of his life and of the Exodus journey. It's a dynamic, ever-evolving story.

In the early days, before the Exodus, Moses is the leader of a dissident group of slaves. He represents them before Pharaoh and demands better conditions and their freedom. Eventually, he leads them out of Egypt, across the Red Sea and into the wilderness.

Now Moses has to exercise a different form of leadership. He has the responsibility of providing for people's needs in the desert wanderings and of ordering their common life. He holds them together and prevents some from creeping back into Egypt. He has to cope with murmurings, grumbling and rebellion. He has to build a nation and settle disputes. Later in the narrative his role will change again as the people prepare for entry into the promised land.

The story told in Exodus 18 marks the transition from the first to the second phase of Moses' leadership. The Red Sea is behind the Israelites now. God has provided manna and quails and water from the rock. There is a pillar of cloud to guide them by day and a pillar of fire by night. But Moses' role still needs to change. Charismatic and heroic leadership has been a key part of the story so far: Moses has been the one through whom God has done great things and because of this the Israelites have followed him. However, the skills needed to lead the slaves out of Egypt are no longer sufficient for the journey through the promised land.

It is at this point that Jethro, Moses' father-in-law, comes to visit. Jethro is a priest of Midian. He worships different gods. As such he stands as an example in Scripture of the role people of different faiths can play in bringing wisdom to the Jewish and to the Christian community. Jethro's gift is principally to listen and to watch what is happening in the community. First he listens carefully to the whole story of the Exodus from Egypt and sits and eats with Moses and Aaron and the elders of Israel. So far so good.

The next day he simply stands around watching what is happening, loitering with intent. Moses sits as judge for the people while the people stand around him from morning to evening.

> When Moses' father-in-law saw all that he was doing for the people he said, 'What is this that you are doing for the people? Why do you sit alone, while all the people stand around you from morning to evening?' (18.14)

Often the people who help us most and can help us to change are those who come from outside, who will sit and listen and watch and ask seemingly innocent questions – perhaps the questions no-one else will dare to ask.

As we all tend to do, Moses defends his own actions. There is more than a hint of how indispensable he has become. As I imagine the dialogue, the 'me' and the 'I' are underlined:

> Moses said to his father-in-law, 'Because the people come to me to inquire of God. When they have a dispute, they come to me and I decide between one person and another, and I make known to them the statutes and instructions of God.' (18.15–16)

But Jethro can see that this pattern is no longer sustainable. It may have been necessary for a time but now it will lead to disaster for Moses and for the new nation:

> Moses' father-in-law said to him, 'What you are doing is not good. You will surely wear yourself out, both you and these people with you. For the task is too heavy for you; you cannot do it alone.' (18.17)

Note the power of Jethro's analysis: the present situation is bad for the leader and bad for the organization. It's a common experience in many kinds of organization. Many leaders wear themselves out and wear out their organization as well. Nothing is flourishing. Something must be done. But what?

Jethro's advice

Jethro's value lies not only in daring to diagnose the problem. He also offers a remarkably succinct and precise solution. The steps now taken are described again at the beginning of the Book of Deuteronomy (though Jethro is not named there). Clearly they are seen as a key development in the life of the nation. However, neither Exodus nor Deuteronomy were written simply to tell a story. These texts are the medium for carrying forward wisdom about leadership in communities from one generation to another. Power must be distributed. Work must be shared. Healthy communities do not happen by accident. They are created by teams of people, working together.

There are three steps to Jethro's prescription. Each is relevant to the exercise of leadership today in many different organizations.

Step 1: Vision and Values

> Now listen to me and I will give you counsel, and God be with you. You should represent the people before God, and you should bring their cases before God; teach them the statutes and instructions and make known to them the way they are to go and the things they are to do. (18.19–20)

Moses cannot do all that he is doing at this stage in the life of the nation. The first stage in delegation is to distinguish between those things he is able to delegate to others and those things only Moses can do at this next stage. At a first reading, the story of Jethro seems to be a simple story about the importance of delegation. However, Jethro is also very clear about defining the role of Moses at this point in the journey: about what cannot be delegated (and is being lost in the constant queues of people seeking guidance).

At this point in the Exodus narrative, Moses has a clear responsibility. He must represent the people before God in prayer and keep alive the vision that they are called in a special way to be

God's people, journeying through the wilderness to a new home in the promised land. He is also called to teach the values of the new community, about to be revealed on Mount Sinai. Teaching these values will provide a common standard and ethic across the community and will itself make possible the delegation and settling of disputes.

A leader is defined as someone people follow. One of the primary requirements of a leader is to have and to hold a clear sense of vision and direction and to keep that vision before the whole community at all times. The vision may be generated in a whole range of ways involving listening and consultation. It will be communicated in all kinds of ways by many different people. But once that vision is clear, it is the very heart of the leader's calling to be the keeper of the vision from year to year and in all the changes and events which happen. This is one of the key tasks which cannot be delegated. It is the central calling of leadership.

The values or ethics of an organization or community are also the key province of the senior leader. This is where the culture, soul or heart of the organization is cherished and formed. A primary calling of senior leadership is to teach those values. Values are always taught in an organization by what St Benedict calls 'a twofold teaching': first by deeds and then by words.

> Therefore whenever anyone receives the name of 'abbot' he is to govern his disciples by a twofold teaching: namely all that is good and holy he must show forth more by deeds than by words; declaring to receptive disciples the commandments of the Lord in words, but to the hard hearted and the simple minded demonstrating the divine precepts by the example of his deeds.[2]

The foundation of building an effective team in any organization lies in first having a clear vision for the organization and guarding it well, then, second, in forming values around that

---

2 The Rule of Saint Benedict, 2.11, 12.

vision and teaching and living those values as a team. As with most things, it helps to write the vision down and to have a written list of values to name and discuss together. The culture of the organization will then be led by vision and the values will spread through that culture and shape it, led by the senior team.

When I became Bishop of Sheffield in 2009, one of the first requirements was to articulate a clear vision for the future development of the diocese. In the vacancy, the diocese had been through a careful process of listening and reflection and was explicitly seeking that new direction. I had anticipated spending six months to a year in further listening after I took up the post. However, very rapidly the diocese was faced with a number of key decisions about finance and appointments. It was vital to take those decisions mindful of the new direction.

So I wrote down a short vision statement and tested it extensively with the senior team, with groups of clergy and lay leaders, in every forum. It was refined and changed a little through that process and then adopted. For six years now that vision statement has guided us through the adoption of values, the working out of strategy, the making of appointments, the balancing of our common life.

> The Diocese of Sheffield is called to grow a sustainable network of Christ-like, lively and diverse Christian communities in every place, which are effective in making disciples and in transforming our society and God's world.

For leaders who find themselves in a Jethro moment, the first questions to ask are these: 'What is my essential role within the organization at the present time?' and 'Are the vision and values clear?'

Step 2: Appointments

> You should also look for able men among all the people, men who fear God, are trustworthy, and hate dishonest gain; set

such men over them as officers over thousands, hundreds, fifties and tens. (18.21)

A key part of leading a team is, of course, finding the right people. Jethro is very clear in his advice to Moses that this too is a key part of his responsibilities. Jethro offers some clear criteria for appointment: faith and character take priority over skills. Here and in the following verses Jethro offers an embryonic role description. Think of these verses as the distillation of wisdom into a very concise story form. To absorb the wisdom they offer, we need to read them slowly, pondering each word or phrase and then translate them into our own contexts.

From 2004 to 2009, I was the first leader of the national Fresh Expressions team. The vision for the team was to encourage the creation of new forms of church for a changing culture as a normal part of the life of the Church of England and the Methodist Church. I had the immense privilege of being able to recruit my own team from scratch.

That experience reinforced for me the vital importance of making appointments as a key part of leadership. In a small organization we could not carry passengers and we could not afford any mistakes. Each team member had to be able to represent Fresh Expressions well in a whole variety of different contexts. We had to work together well to accomplish an ambitious programme of change. I invested a great deal in designing the roles, in looking for Christians of proven personal maturity, in seeking the right blend of creativity and the mix of gifts and skills across the team. It took a year of hard work to scope the roles, make the appointments and gather everyone together in one place so that we could begin our work together. Over the next four years, what we accomplished together was far greater than the sum of what each of us could accomplish individually. We learned to be a team.

Here again, Jethro's advice is not about relieving Moses of work so that he can be at leisure. Jethro's concise advice highlights the essential places where Moses must focus his energies. After his care for vision and values, the second most important focus must be the design of roles and the appointment of a great senior team.

High-quality appointments in any organization take an immense amount of time from the review and design of the role, through the recruitment process to the induction of the new senior colleague. They cannot be led and managed if the person leading them is constantly swamped and overwhelmed by detail. The modern-day equivalent of the queue of people around Moses from morning to night will be the email inbox or the string of phone messages at the end of the day.

Step 3: Delegate

> Let them sit as judges for the people at all times; let them bring every important case before you, but decide every minor case themselves. So it will be easier for you, and they will bear the burden with you. If you do this, and God so commands you, then you will be able to endure and all these people will go to their home in peace. (18.22–23)

Jethro's third step is the delegation of the non-essential tasks, the routine work of deciding disputes between the people. This is, of course, a different matter from making the right appointments. It is not hard to find leaders who appoint good people but then fail effectively to delegate the routine work to those they have appointed.

Delegation sounds straightforward and in some cases it is. In others it can be surprisingly difficult to let go of a task in such a way that others are set free to do it in their own way but within an overall framework of supervision. Many leaders find it very hard emotionally to delegate tasks to others and keep trying to take back the key decisions for a range of complex reasons. We love to be needed and we love to demonstrate to others that we are needed. It is always interesting to be in a room with people trying to find a time for an important meeting. People will compete to show how busy they are.

The other common mistake is to set people up to fail (which again subtly reinforces our own importance). The way to do this is to delegate completely and offer no support or supervision or moderation of the outcomes. Neither is what Jethro has in mind here.

Jethro advocates a model of delegation within a framework of supervision. Behind it lie three sets of questions which a senior leader needs to answer. The first is to articulate the key principles of subsidiarity. What can be dealt with locally, at the grass roots, is decided there. More complex decisions are referred to the next level. Does everyone understand this? How is it articulated and reviewed?

The second is around how a team meets together and structures its meetings. Again a key part of a leader's responsibility is the design and leading of those gatherings and their pattern over the course of a year. Is there sufficient time for engagement together, for tending to relationships, for routine decision making, grappling with complex problems and for strategic thinking? If the context is one of a Christian organization, is there space for prayer and worship? The team meeting is not only about how the work is done. It is about how the team grow and are nurtured as people and as leaders.

The third is how the leader meets one to one with his or her key reports and what happens in those meetings. Jethro's model pays very careful attention to the span of care. People are appointed over thousands, hundreds, fifties and tens. The normal span of care is therefore one person overseeing ten others. However, there is also a level in the organization where the span of oversight is one to two and those two in turn look after five people. This is, I think, where capacity is created for growing the emerging leaders of the future. How do those supervision meetings operate? Is there time for mutual tending, relationship building, proper scrutiny of decisions and the raising of complex problems in confidence which cannot be brought into a whole team meeting?

Accepting help

Leaders often find themselves living in a paradox. The more responsibility we carry, the more advice and help we need in a complex, ever-changing role. But the more responsibility we carry, the harder it becomes to listen to that advice and help. Trusted companions, external perspectives, humility and open ears are essential to discover what is not working and to mend it.

At each stage of the leadership task, there is a danger that the essential tasks of leadership will be overwhelmed by the detail. In those moments as leaders we need an external perspective, fresh eyes. Those eyes will help us see the essential things we need to do and those which can be delegated to others.

Again and again we will need to remember:

For the task is too heavy for you; you cannot do it alone.

6

Gentleness

Proverbs 15.1–7

*A gentle tongue is a tree of life
but perverseness in it breaks the spirit.*

(15.4)

Choosing words

The words we use are a vital part of our leadership, whatever our role. Leadership is not only about great set speeches or major decisions about vision or direction. Leadership is exercised through face to face meetings and phone conversations, through thousands of emails, through blogs and articles, through the way we answer questions and respond to dissent. Leadership is about influencing others and one of the key ways leaders exercise influence is through our words and the way we use them.

Think of the way a mother speaks to her eight-year-old son or what a head teacher says in the school assembly. Think of the way the CEO speaks to the receptionist on the way into the office. How does a Director of Finance respond to an angry email? How does the local councillor engage with the protests on social media? How does the army officer write to the family of an injured soldier? What does the leader of the local food bank write in the newsletter to encourage volunteers?

People take more notice than we imagine of what we say and the way we say it. For eight years I was responsible for a college where men and women were training for ordained ministry (and for leadership as part of ministry). I took careful notice (of course) of the ways in which they spoke to me and wrote to me. But I learned to take even greater notice of the ways in which they spoke and wrote to the college secretaries and support staff. It was a much better indicator of their effectiveness as leaders in the future.

Good text books on leadership will often have chapters and sometimes whole sections on communication. But often the focus will be on the more visible skills: how to write an effective speech, perhaps, or the importance of a presence on social media. Where should a leader turn when looking for something deeper?

Wisdom

There is a strand in the great library of the Bible which goes by the name of Wisdom Literature. Proverbs is the main example. Job and Ecclesiastes also belong to a later part of this tradition and so do some of the psalms. There are other collections in the Apocrypha: Ecclesiasticus and the Wisdom of Solomon. The closest New Testament book to this tradition is the Letter of James. If you search outside Israel, there are parallel Wisdom traditions in Egypt and in other parts of the ancient Near East.

The wise in ancient Israel were the teachers: those responsible for the education of the young and those responsible for the education of future leaders in different walks of life – especially the scribes or secretaries, the civil servants who would govern the nation in every generation. The Wisdom Literature takes us deeper than the dramas of the lives of the kings and the royal court to the practice and habits of more ordinary, everyday leadership.

These scribes or wise teachers prized words and the careful use of words. They had no use at all for long text books or abstract treatises on leadership. They loved stories with a meaning. It's likely that the stories in the history books of Samuel and Kings were collected in the wisdom schools around the temple and used in teaching each generation of new leaders.

The wisdom teachers also prized short, memorable sayings, pregnant with meaning and wit, known as riddles or proverbs. These sayings would be copied out, learned by heart, treasured from generation to generation, used as a basis of conversation and discussion. In that way, they would form the lives of the godly scribes of the future. They are a deep repository of wisdom on leadership in communities. The Book of Proverbs is the primary collection in the Bible of this great tradition. Whenever you are reading a section of Proverbs, wherever the text says 'wisdom' read this as 'wisdom in leadership' (for that is really what the text means). There is a huge resource for reflection here.

The power of words

Take a moment to read the first seven verses of Proverbs 15:

A soft answer turns away wrath,
but a harsh word stirs up anger.
The tongue of the wise dispenses knowledge,
but the mouths of fools pour out folly.
The eyes of the LORD are in every place,
keeping watch on the evil and the good.
A gentle tongue is a tree of life,
but perverseness in it breaks the spirit.
A fool despises a parent's instruction,
but the one who heeds admonition is prudent.
In the house of the righteous there is much treasure,
but trouble befalls the income of the wicked.
The lips of the wise spread knowledge;
not so the minds of fools. (15.1–7)

You will see that reflecting on the use of words is a key part of wisdom on leadership. Five of the seven sayings here are reflections on how people use words: on how to answer anger; on whose words to hear and attend to and so on. Each one repays careful reflection. Studying a good proverb is a little like savouring a fine wine or clicking on an icon on your tablet. There is a world of meaning underneath the words.

This careful use of words is underlined by the careful, poetic way in which the individual Proverbs are constructed. Hebrew poetry works not through rhyme but through repetition: saying the same thing (or opposite things) in the two halves of a verse. That same poetic device is carried across to the wisdom sayings. It makes them easy to remember and full of flavour.

So let's think together for a moment about Proverbs 15.4 and its meaning for leaders of all kinds: 'A gentle tongue is a tree of life, but perverseness in it breaks the spirit.' What might these words mean and what difference should they make?

Let's begin with the way the verse draws attention to the immense power of words to shape lives. In the biblical tradition of leadership, words are weighty, important, potentially life giving and soul destroying. They can do immense good and they can do great damage.

This is the opposite of the way in which our own culture thinks about words. There are so many words around us all the time. We not only have printed books but newspapers, the internet, online publications, Twitter, a constant stream of words flowing towards us and within us and from us. We screen out many of these words. We know that many are untrue or inaccurate. The currency of words is debased.

Most of us also have running around deep within us a proverb from our own culture which is the very opposite of Proverbs 15.4:

Sticks and stones may break my bones but words will never hurt me.

This seems to imply that words are light, ineffective and neutral things which can do little damage (and by implication, little that is good).

We need to begin then by taking words in general, and our own words, much more seriously. Most of us would be honest enough to admit that words can be damaging and hurtful, especially if repeated over time by those we love and respect. The modern saying about sticks and stones actually runs counter to a major strand of teaching in the whole of the Bible.

According to the Scriptures, words, quite literally, shape the universe. If you read or remember Genesis 1 and the account of creation, God creates by the spoken word. The Psalms and the Prophets bear witness to the power of words through beautiful imagery and poetry: words shape the world and give meaning to our lives. In the New Testament, Jesus himself, God's Son, is described in John's gospel as the Word made flesh. It is hard to overestimate the importance of words in both experience and in the scriptures. They create wonder and depth in life.

Our proverb balances the two opposite effects that words can have. One kind of word offered and given is a tree of life. This is an image drawn from the Garden of Eden, from paradise. It's a dynamic image. Careful creative words are not only a blessing to the person to whom they are spoken: those words become in them a means of blessing to others and so on down the ages. But words which are twisted and hurtful have the opposite effect: they break the spirit, the very core, of a person and mean that they are unable to find their own potential and unable to be a blessing to others in their life and work.

Gentleness in leadership

The words leaders use are important therefore. What is the most important quality in the way we use the words we are given? Proverbs 15.4 suggests that quality is gentleness: that Christian leaders should be gentle in what they say. In so far as we embody gentleness in our words and in our tongue, we will enable others to be bearers of life to others. Conversely, perverseness in what we say to others will damage those whom we are called to lead.

Gentleness is a deeply Christian quality in understanding leadership. The Old Testament does have an understanding of power which manifests itself in feats of arms and oratory and accomplishment. However, over the course of the Bible, this understanding of power gives way to another tradition: that of the gentle leader. Nowhere is this clearer than in the prophecy of Isaiah 40–55.

These chapters are thought by most scholars to be the work of a prophet of the Exile, living in Babylon and working within the great tradition of Isaiah of Jerusalem. This prophet describes himself only as 'a voice' crying in the wilderness. My own name for him is 'Col' from the Hebrew meaning 'voice' (but others call him by his longer name of Second Isaiah).

Col is preaching to the exiles, preparing them for the moment when God will lead them home. He weaves into his prophecy four beautiful songs which all focus on the nature of leadership. They are called the Servant Songs because they speak of the servant of the Lord who is coming to redeem God's people and lead them home. Right at the heart of Col's understanding of what it means to be a leader and to wield power is an understanding of gentleness.

> He will not cry or lift up his voice or make it heard in the street
> A bruised reed he will not break and a dimly burning wick he will not quench,
> He will faithfully bring forth justice.
> He will not faint or grow weary
> Until he has established justice in the earth. (42.2–4)

Gentleness in leadership is expressed in decisions and actions, of course, but it is mediated primarily through words. An effective leader in a school, a church, an office, will probably be marked out most clearly by gentleness. It is this quality which will give life and enable others to be a tree of life. It is the very opposite of what some literature means by leadership.

Power tempered by gentleness

Why is gentleness of speech such a vital characteristic in those called to leadership? This has a great deal to do with the way in which we exercise power in communities.

Most leaders have moments when they become aware of the way their words are heard by others. For me, this has almost always happened in moments of transition. I'm not, naturally, a person who takes his own words and actions too seriously. It came as a considerable surprise, therefore, that when I became the Warden of a theological college, I noticed that people in the community took what I said, most of the time, very seriously.

This was because my position as a leader in that community had the effect of amplifying my words and, especially, amplifying any harshness or sharpness in them. My leadership role meant that my words somehow had increased power both to build up but also to do harm. They could be a tree of life but they could also break the spirit. The power and authority of my position in the community had to be tempered with gentleness for that power to be exercised safely and wisely.

The Rule of Benedict, one of the earliest guides to monastic life, captures this sense of gentleness in community in a beautiful phrase in the Prologue. The Rule is intended to establish 'a school of the Lord's service'. Benedict continues: 'In instituting it we hope to establish nothing harsh or oppressive'. The Latin is even better: 'nihil asperum, nihil grave' – literally nothing sharp and nothing heavy.[1] This is the kind of speech which gives life in communities.

---

1 The Rule of Benedict, Prologue, 46–7.

When the news was announced that I was to be made Bishop of Sheffield, I received a very large number of cards and emails. I think the most precious one of all was from Richard Hare, for many years Bishop of Pontefract in the Diocese of Wakefield, where I grew up and served as a vicar for nine years. Richard had known me since I was fifteen, watched over me as an ordinand and a curate, had been my bishop in my first incumbency and had kept in touch down the years of his retirement with me and a large number of his other ordinands. He was then 86 and in poor health and died the following year.

In his email, Richard described advice given to him by his own friend and mentor, William Greer, one time Bishop of Manchester, at the time of Richard's own consecration as a bishop. Greer was too frail to attend the service and so Richard, his former chaplain, visited him a day or so before:

> It was a warm, sunny, September day and he was sitting in a deck chair in the garden. He knew I would remember what he said for the rest of my life and I am sure he had spent the morning deciding what it should be. We sat in silence for a while and then it came: 'The most important thing for a bishop to learn is how to increase his gentleness.' That was 37 years ago and I can truthfully say there has never been a day when I have not been conscious of what William Greer said in the garden at Woodland that morning.

Gentle words

It is not only bishops who need to increase in gentleness daily. It is a necessary part of every form of leadership. Paul writes to the Philippians: 'Let your gentleness be known to everyone' (4.5).

Leadership is about enabling individuals and communities, businesses and organizations to flourish. Flourishing is about becoming the best you can be, bearing fruit, being a tree of life.

Words are vital in that process. Words are able to inspire, to teach, to impart courage, to pass on instructions, to impart an ethos and a way of doing things. But the greatest gift of all in the way we use words is gentleness.

For many, if not all of us, this proverb and William Greer's words create a challenge. We find it hard to understand the effect of the words we use and harder still to control and moderate them with gentleness. That challenge is meant to be there. Gentleness is a fruit of the Holy Spirit's work in our lives as we are formed over time into the likeness of Christ (see Galatians 5.23). To grow in holiness is also to grow in the exercise of leadership.

7

Chaos

Genesis 1.1–2.4

*In the beginning when God created the heavens
and the earth, the earth was a formless void and
darkness covered the face of the deep, while a wind
from God swept over the face of the waters.*

(1.1–2)

When everything is falling apart . . .

Leadership is always demanding but some leadership roles do feel routine and straightforward. The organization is running well. The vision is clear. There are no storms in view. The task from year to year is to go on doing what you are doing and to make incremental improvements. Other leadership roles may feel more demanding than this. Everyone acknowledges there are serious issues to address. There is a need for root and branch review but at least the overall direction is clear and some parts are working.

But a third kind of leadership task feels much more testing. The organization is in crisis. There are no resources. The wrong people are in the wrong kinds of roles. You are one bad decision away from a disaster. So many problems face the leaders that it is hard to know where to begin. To use that well-known biblical image, the writing is on the wall.

This kind of diagnosis can apply to a local authority department, a hospital, a school, a charity or a church. Where should

Christian leaders turn for inspiration when faced with this kind of challenge?

The normal text books on leadership don't give much space to how to lead when the very fabric of the organization is falling apart. They are mostly concerned with incremental development or helping to make a good organization better. I suspect this is partly because most of them have emerged from reflections on leadership in a commercial context. An unprofitable company will simply disappear over time and another will take its place. Although the human consequences of that change will be difficult, the leadership challenge is clearer.

However, in the charitable sector or in the health service, in education or in the church these constraints do not apply. If a medium-sized town is served by a single further education college and that college is poorly governed and badly run, the town will be blighted for a generation. The person who is appointed to lead the college has to have the aim of turning things around, over time. The challenges are more real and much more demanding for the leader. The same would be true in a GP surgery, a parish church, a failing primary school, or a hospice. A very large number of leaders will face this kind of situation over the course of their working lives. We are called to lead in times of chaos. When that challenge happens, where do you begin?

Order out of chaos

Let's start at the very beginning. There are two accounts of the creation of the world in the early chapters of the Book of Genesis (and several others scattered through the Bible). Neither is meant as a detailed literal and historical account of how the world was made. Both are affirming deep truths about the universe and about God's work in creation. The first creation story in Genesis 1.1–2.4 has a great deal to teach us about leadership.

Genesis 1 is not an account of creation out of nothing. Rather, God is shaping and ordering the world. The place the story begins is not in the time when nothing existed at all. We need to read the first verses of John's gospel for that perspective. Here the earth is a formless void. The Hebrew expression, *tohu wa bohu* means an expanse of nothingness. One of the early Greek translations means 'shapeless'. God creates the world from chaos. Take a moment to imagine what that chaos might have looked like: the earth without form, and empty.

The great symbol of chaos in the Bible (and in the ancient Near East) is water: the vast expanse of the sea. In the modern world we can have a romantic and positive view of the sea but that was not so in the Bible. Wherever the sea occurs it is a symbol of chaos and darkness and death. Think of the flood story later in Genesis when creation is undone and destroyed. Think of the crossing of the Red Sea in the Exodus where the Israelites are delivered and saved but the Egyptian army is overwhelmed. Think of the story of Jonah and his song from the belly of the fish:

'You cast me into the deep,
into the heart of the seas,
and the floods surrounded me;
all your waves and billows passed over me.' (Jonah 2.3)

In Genesis 1.1 God's Spirit (the same word in Hebrew as wind) is brooding over the face of the waters. We are not told how long this brooding, hovering or sweeping over the waters took. But when the creation begins it is a story of bringing order out of chaos before anything new is made. God brings order first through separating out one thing from another. The light is separated from the darkness and God names the light and darkness. God separates the sky from the earth and the dry ground from the sea and gives them names.

This principle of bringing good order continues through the creation story. There is a careful order to the creation of first plants, then fish and birds and finally humankind as the pinnacle of creation. There is a careful delineation of time into days and each day into the evening and the morning. In contrast to our modern, Western view of time, the evening is the beginning of the day (when we rest and enjoy God's creation) and the morning comes second (when we awake and join our work to what God is already doing). The high point of the creation story is the gift of the Sabbath: the day of rest and reflection which gives meaning to the whole. God's leadership is rooted in bringing fruitful order out of chaos.

Brooding

If most of our models of leadership are drawn from the world of commerce and business, it is not, perhaps, surprising that they are dominated by images of growth and a desire for the organization to become larger and more profitable. Projections and trajectories abound. The shaping question for leadership is, 'How do I help this organization to grow and become larger and more profitable?'

These images and questions are helpful and necessary in most contexts. But, in many, we need another set of questions and models to set alongside them. In many different contexts we should be striving not for growth but to bring fruitful order out of chaos. This leadership task is much more like the work of God in Genesis 1. As we will see, it has to do with a kind of holy and loving brooding over the face of the deep – facing and pondering the many different issues and questions which confront you. It has to do with discerning the right place to begin: the first problem to tackle which will help you tackle all the others. It has to do with separating out the dry land from the waters: finding places where there can be creative and fruitful development in the midst of a host of different problems. It has something to do with carrying the longer perspective: of understanding what you are trying to create, of the length of time it will take, of the value of persevering through the demanding early years of reconstruction until fruitful and creative growth begins again.

There are two key skills which leaders need in these situations. They are habits and dispositions of character as well as skills. The first is captured by the phrase: 'The Spirit of God brooded over the face of the deep' (Genesis 1.1 in the Authorized Version). Leaders faced with chaotic organizations need to brood. The second is the ability to understand and to shape time creatively and well.

Brooding has several different strands of meaning. It means first to have the patience and courage to dwell with and within the chaos, to explore the complexity and to attempt to understand the context well. This takes considerable courage and patience. All leaders do well to remember that to every complex problem there is a simple solution and it is nearly always wrong. In particular leaders must do everything they can not to assume that now that the right leader has arrived (themselves), sorting this mess out will be very straightforward. It takes time to understand a new situation really well and to live within it.

Second, to brood means to take the second vital step of making time and space to think and reflect before acting. A leader who does not make time to reflect when addressing chaos will certainly be overwhelmed. We all reflect in a myriad different ways. However, the capacity to journal, to discuss the situation with others, to take time away with a core team, to retreat, will be absolutely vital in making progress.

Third, to brood means to love. The more difficult and challenging a situation, the more the people within it will need love and care and commitment from those entrusted with leadership. The English word brood comes from the image of a hen sitting on a nest of eggs. Christians believe that God made the world in love. Love is a vital part of any kind of leadership but especially leadership from chaos.

And fourth, brooding implies patience and discernment not only about where to begin but also about when to act. We are not told how long the Spirit of God was brooding over the face of the waters but the implication is that this was not a matter of moments. There was a season of planning, reflection, preparation, before the decisive beginning was made. The greater the chaos, the harder it will be to wait. There may be a need to triage the problems and to deal with urgent presenting issues rapidly. But the deeper, systemic work of brooding will need longer.

Managing time

The second key skill which leaders need when facing situations of chaos is one of the great sub-themes of the chapter. An essential part of the act of bringing order from chaos is the ability to understand, to divide, to order and to manage time. A very significant number of leaders struggle most in our lives with the right ordering of time and energy.

Genesis 1 sets the very creation of the universe within a framework of the ordering of time into night and day, evening and morning and seven great 'days' of creation. The last of them is, of course, the day of rest, reflection, review and recreation, the gift of Sabbath:

So God blessed the seventh day and hallowed it, because on it God rested from all the work that he had done in creation. (Genesis 2.3)

Leadership always involves the ordering of time for the leader themselves and, often, for other people. As a College Principal, one of my most important tasks was drawing up and reflecting on the timetable. Should breakfast be before or after Morning

Prayer? How long should we allow for lunch and coffee? Should certain days be kept clear and free for study or prayer? What are the principles and habits by which time needs to be ordered in healthy institutions?

The first, counter-cultural insight is that rest should find an honoured place in the rhythm of the week, the day and the year. Human beings cannot work all the time. We become less than human if we attempt to do so (or if we attempt to make others do so). Organizations and communities need rest, fallow periods, down time for healing and mending and reflection and to be recreated. Leaders need to have an eye always to the work levels of the communities they serve. The temptation will sometimes be to run too fast rather than walk too slowly.

One of the most influential documents in the history of Western civilization is the Rule of Benedict. The Rule has shaped not only monastic and church life but the life of universities and schools, hospitals and whole societies. Much of the Rule is taken up with the proper ordering of time: the hours of the day, the days of the week and the seasons of the year. Benedict shapes time in a humane way so that a community which follows the Rule gives the right time and priority to prayer, to rest and to work (in that order of priority). Benedict is drawing on profound insights in creation. What were men and women made for? We were not made to be units of production. We were not made only to work. We were created for friendship and relationship with God – to know and enjoy God for ever – and for community.

The second is that time needs to be ordered so that the right energy and attention is given to each element of the task over the course of a week, a month, a year. Not all times are the same. The created world has its seasons. These seasons give a rhythm to the year. In John 15, Jesus implies, in his picture of the vine, that the life of the Christian community and the disciple is also seasonal. Periods of great fruitfulness will alternate with a sense of being pruned and abiding more deeply in the vine.

A wise leader will constantly reflect on the way in which their own time is ordered and on the ordering of time in the community. Is enough time being spent in nurturing the team, in tending the life of the community, in outward-facing activity? Are people able to rest and be replenished in the normal rhythms of the week? Is everything running just slightly too fast for people's good? Or is there a need for more momentum and greater energy? How can adjusting the timetable and the culture of the organization impact the wellbeing of those who work within it and those whom the organization serves?

Leadership in a crisis

One of the great examples of a leader bringing order out of chaos in the Bible is the story of Nehemiah. Nehemiah is charged with leadership in his community in a time of great crisis. The exiles have returned from Babylon but things are not going well. There are no walls or gates around Jerusalem. Everything is in chaos.

Nehemiah broods over the news from the exiles. His brooding turns to prayer and a sense of responsibility. His sense of responsibility becomes a call to action and the King agrees to his request to send him to Jerusalem to rebuild the city. His first task when he arrives is more watching and looking: the inspection of the walls. He realizes the first thing that must be done: the rebuilding of the walls. This is necessary for the security of the people, to define their boundaries, to raise their self-esteem, to draw them together.

Nehemiah calls them to the task and he galvanizes them by his example. When a group face a huge number of tasks, the most important task of leadership is to bring vision which helps to order priorities. Nehemiah then brings order to the work by assigning to each family a section of wall so that it can all be built at once and swiftly. He is alert to the dangers and sets a guard so that the work can continue even in times of difficulty. The building is carried out in a context of multiple threats and difficulties.

The building of the wall is simply the beginning of the rebuilding of the nation. Once that task has been completed, a new problem emerges, and then another. Rebuilding from chaos is like that. Nehemiah adjusts his role, his priorities, his time as one milestone is reached and another horizon appears. It is rarely the task of a single leader to complete the rebuilding of an entire organization. This is a long-term task and one person hands on the baton to another.

But one of the features the Book of Nehemiah has in common with the first chapter of Genesis is the sense of progress. God looks back on the seventh day, according to Genesis, and surveys the whole of creation, the bringing of order from chaos. Nehemiah looks back at the end of his service in Jerusalem and sees the progress which has been made in reconstruction. So one of the most fulfilling parts of leadership is to look back from time to time, to see the progress which has been made and to rejoice and give thanks for the new life and order and fruitfulness which have emerged.

8

Covenant

Ruth

Where you go, I will go;
where you lodge, I will lodge;
your people will be my people,
and your God my God.

(1.16)

Commitment

I've always remembered something one of my colleagues said to me early in our working relationship. I was a vicar at the time and he was one of my curates, newly arrived from college to spend the first years of his ministry working with me. I was anxious about this new relationship (as I normally am) and it probably showed. My new colleague made a short speech at one of our first meetings which set the tone for our time together. He said, very simply, 'I am here to put my shoulder to your wheel.' It was a simple promise of loyalty and commitment and it became the foundation of an excellent working relationship from which I learned as much if not more than did my colleague.

Leading any organization demands team work. Working together in teams demands multiple skills. However, the foundation of working together as colleagues is mutual commitment to one another of loyalty, respect and love. The Bible calls this kind of commitment a covenant: a solemn, life-shaping and potentially world-shaping agreement.

There are many leadership lessons in the great HBO drama, the West Wing, about the fictional President Bartlett and his team of staff. One of the very best comes at the end of Bartlett's second inauguration as President. His team have worked together through thick and thin to produce an outstanding election result and a brilliant inauguration speech. After the speech, Bartlett appoints one of its authors, Will Bailey, to a permanent role within his team and says this:

Bartlett: There's a promise that I ask everyone who works here to make: never doubt that a small group of thoughtful and committed citizens can change the world. You know why?

Will: It's the only thing that ever has.[1]

One of the foundations of great leadership is the forging of covenants and alliances: combining our energy, vision, commitment and gifts with those of others who share our values to bring about lasting change.

Ruth

One of the greatest studies of this kind of covenant between individuals in the Bible is the Book of Ruth. At first reading the story of Ruth feels rather domestic. In the English Bible, Ruth is sandwiched between the great historical narratives of Joshua and Samuel. We move from the vast sweep of history and the clashes of nations to the affairs of a single family. In the Hebrew Bible Ruth is placed after Proverbs and grouped with other shorter books which alerts us rather better to its significance.

---

1 Aaron Sorkin, *The West Wing*, Season 4, Inauguration, Part II.

Ruth does tell the story of one extended family at a particular moment in their lives: the key action of the book takes place over a few months. The characters are caught up in the dramas of their day but they are not in any sense leaders: they are not prophets or priests, kings or queens.

But actually the Book of Ruth is entirely focused on leadership and the foundations of leadership. To see this clearly you need to read right to the end of the book. At the end of the story, Naomi has a grandson, born to Ruth and Boaz:

> They named him Obed; he became the father of Jesse, the father of David. (4.17)

The greatest of Israel's kings emerged from the family whose story is told here. Jesus Christ himself, from the line of David, claims Ruth as his ancestor (and Ruth is mentioned by name in the genealogy in Matthew 1). It is not difficult to imagine the story of Ruth being passed down within the family of Boaz and Obed and Jesse, as indeed it was passed down within the whole nation of Israel. The foundation of families, of teams, of leadership, of an entire nation, are the virtues of loyalty and faithfulness: covenant.

Migrants

There is a famine in Bethlehem and so a man and his wife and their two sons move to the neighbouring country of Moab. The woman is Naomi. Her husband dies in Moab. Her two sons take wives from that country. Then after ten years, Naomi's two sons die also. Her life is blighted by these three tragedies. She is far from home.

Naomi hears that the famine has ended in Israel and so she prepares to return. She urges her two daughters-in-law to remain among their own people. Three times she says to them: 'Go back . . . turn back . . . turn back' and gives them her blessing. The first, Orpah, eventually returns. Naomi seeks to send Ruth away a fourth time. But Ruth joins herself to Naomi and

to the people of God in one of the greatest moments of the whole
drama of the Old Testament:

> 'Do not press me to leave you
> or to turn back from following you!
> Where you go, I will go;
> where you lodge, I will lodge;
> Your people shall be my people,
> and your God my God.
> Where you die, I will die –
> there I will be buried.
> May the LORD do thus and so to me,
> and more as well,
> if even death parts me from you!' (Ruth 1.16–17)

Ruth makes a covenant – a solemn promise and vow of loyalty
which will shape her life from this day forwards. The covenant
made by Ruth is both risky and sacrificial. It would be the safer
course for Ruth to remain with her kindred in Moab than risk
a long journey and a life of poverty with her mother-in-law in a
foreign land. These were dangerous times to be without security
and protection.

Yet these two women are immeasurably stronger because of
their commitment and friendship, their covenant across the generations. Together they begin to have the strength and resources
to reshape their lives and to shape the world. Naomi offers to
Ruth her wisdom, advice and wider network of friends. Ruth
offers to Naomi her loyalty and love, her labour and her trust.
Naomi's life seems to have come to an end. Ruth is a stranger
and a migrant. Yet the alliance between them creates possibili-
ties of resilience and change. They are colleagues in the rebuilding of their lives, their home and their family. Naomi's wisdom
and Ruth's courage combine with the generosity and goodness
of Boaz to set a new and strong foundation for what will become
the House of Jesse and the line of Israel's kings.

The story carries many lessons in leadership and forming leaders. In particular, the story helps us to see the value of forming and sustaining different kinds of strong relationships which lie at the heart of every common endeavour. We will explore those lessons through the themes of being mentored, mentoring others and forming teams.

Finding your mentor

Ruth is at a moment in her life when she needs an anchor, great wisdom and strong support. She has been widowed as a young adult. Her life lies ahead of her. On the road back to Bethlehem she faces one of the great vocational choices of her life: to continue the adventure to Bethlehem or to return to her old family and tribe and life and remain in Moab. Which will it be?

The friendship and guidance of someone who cares for her, who has her best interests at heart, is of inestimable value to Ruth's life both in the crisis on the road to Bethlehem and in helping Ruth to navigate through the early months in Bethlehem and supporting her family in the years to come (for Naomi becomes nurse to her son).

Countless young leaders in many different walks of life stand in need of friendship, advice and support today. That advice is needed in the major vocational decisions about key life and career choices. It is needed in response to crises of different kinds. It is needed in the smaller details of strategy and navigating through new roles and situations.

In every walk of life, leaders who are Christians have a huge resource available to them in the inestimable gift of the community of the Church. In contemporary society, local church congregations are one of the few key meeting places between the generations. In the wider family of the Church are vital resources for mutual support between Christian leaders in life's major choices and in the minor setbacks. This local community can, in turn, open up wider networks of mutual support based on shared values.

The wider community of the Church, through ministers, religious houses, networks and conferences, is a huge potential source of support and mentoring. There are immense resources in the Christian traditions of spiritual direction and vocational guidance to support leaders in making key decisions and offering support. All too often these resources are not being used. Young Christian leaders do not realize the immense treasures available to them in the Christian community and the potential which is unlocked through discovering them.

The workplace too can be a place where long-lasting mentoring and coaching relationships are formed. Key questions for every leader in any kind of organization must be, 'Where am I able to quarry the strength and support I need for the leadership role to which I am called? Where are the key relationships inside and outside the workplace which will offer wisdom and love in the decisions which will need to be taken? Where are those who will help me learn and grow in this new situation?' Again and again, leadership fails because leaders attempt Herculean tasks in isolation.

One of the key learning points in leadership is learning to take responsibility for forming these relationships with those who will be our mentors and senior colleagues. Most of us begin the journey of leadership by projecting onto others the responsibility for ensuring that we, ourselves, are mentored and supported. These relationships are something that should be arranged and offered by the organization we work within, we think. Or else older and wiser people should simply go out of their way to befriend and support us (perhaps as we would like to do for others).

But organizations and people are imperfect and have a finite amount of time and energy. The leaders who are most likely to have the support they need are those who take responsibility for this aspect of their lives, who look for support and who, once they have found it, take care to develop it. They are the people who have the humility and courage to find spiritual directors, senior friends and work consultants and who will say to them, 'May we travel together and may I learn from you as we go?'

Ruth saw something in Naomi on the road to Bethlehem: a combination of faith, courage in adversity, enduring love. Ruth understood in the moment of her decision that these qualities were life forming and life shaping and for those reasons Ruth clung to Naomi and followed her into an unknown future. Who are the people who help you set your course and find your bearings in the leadership you offer?

Mentoring others

In the same way, it is good to ask at every stage of life and leadership, who are the people whom you are seeking to mentor and develop? Whose career are you seeking to guide? In whose character and life are you investing your own life? In every field, raising up a new generation of leaders is part of the vocation of leadership.

For many in leadership, there will be opportunities to do this in the workplace and in the organization. Sometimes this will be recognized and sometimes it will be informal. The story of Naomi and Ruth teaches us that it is not always the case that the mentor and the mentee share a common faith (though increasingly they will share at least some values). Ruth was of the religion of Moab until her confession on the Bethlehem road.

For many there will (or could) be many ways to offer this kind of mentoring and support through the local church community. At every stage of line, small groups and one-to-one conversations offer this kind of key support. Churches are not simply places where we go to worship or to learn the Christian faith. They are vital communities where life-shaping friendships are formed, covenants made for a time and sometimes for life, and where wisdom for life is imparted.

Naomi's story teaches us a vital lesson in mentoring others. The goal of the exercise is the flourishing of the person being mentored, not the needs of the mentor. The object is not to create others in our own likeness. Nor is it to see people grow for the benefits they can bring to the organization. The best mentoring and development conversations are based on generosity. The object is to see individuals flourish and grow fully into the people God intends them to be. Mentoring others is essentially a generous activity within a covenant framework of mutual support.

Trust

There are many books about working in teams. One of the best and most widely read is Patrick Lencioni's parable, *The Five Dysfunctions of a Team*.[2] Lencioni begins from the premise that working in teams is challenging and difficult. Whilst team work holds great potential for any kind of organization, often that potential is not realized.

The first and most fundamental of Lencioni's five dysfunctions is absence of trust. People find it hard to work together because we do not trust each other. The second is fear of conflict (which flows, of course, from absence of trust). The third is lack of commitment to one another and to the task. It is not hard to see the relevance of Ruth and Naomi's story to the formation of strong and effective teams in which everyone flourishes. They are built from strong relationships between people who are committed to one another, know and understand each other and seek the common good.

Throughout my working life, it has been a privilege normally to work in teams. I've been a member of, and a leader of, teams of ministers in different parishes. I've worked within and rebuilt a team of tutors in a college, set up and led a national dispersed

2 Patrick Lencioni, *The Five Dysfunctions of a Team*, San Francisco, CA: Jossey Bass, 2002.

team to encourage fresh expressions of church and reshaped a senior leadership team in a diocese.

Each of those teams has been built (or rebuilt) through forming strong relationships of trust with people as individuals: knowing their stories, their values, their strengths and weaknesses. These one-to-one relationships are vital. From that foundation, it is possible to seek to grow a healthy relationship and shared values across the team.

One of the common errors I see in teams in a church context (and outside the church) is that people will often spend time in meetings but very little time in one-to-one conversations and reviews. Both are vital – and good teams don't happen without forming habits of one-to-one engagement alongside the time together.

As you read and reflect on the story of Ruth, reflect on the covenants you have made in your working life and, perhaps, on those you need to make. Are the people you work most closely with aware of your commitment to them and your support for them? Are you well supported by those who mentor you and seek to grow your leadership? If not, how can you take responsibility for that situation and set up better structures for your own growth? Are you actively mentoring and supporting the next generation of leaders and investing in them? What are you doing to spend time one-to-one with those you work most closely with?

Never doubt, says President Bartlett, that a small group of thoughtful and committed citizens can change the world. What change do you want to see through the leadership you offer? What are you doing to forge small groups of thoughtful and committed citizens who covenant together to bring this change about?

9

Change

1 Samuel 7.15–8.22

You are old and your sons do not follow in your ways;
appoint for us, then, a king to govern us, like other nations.

(8.5)

Friendship with God

Samuel lived almost all his life in a dialogue with God. This dialogue began when he was very young. I remember as a child first hearing the story of how Samuel heard God's voice at the age of seven. I wondered then about how my own friendship with God might begin. But the long conversation between Samuel and the Lord continues well into adult life and old age. In 1 Samuel 8 we get to listen in on that conversation. Samuel and God are able to say hard things to one another and talk over their response to rejection. This intimacy does not happen without a very, very long friendship.

One of the distinctive qualities and gifts Christians bring to the task of leadership and influencing others is a life which is shaped by prayer. Prayer is, of course, about much more than asking God for things on our own behalf or on behalf of others. Prayer is at the heart of a living relationship, a friendship, in which God calls us to walk closely in communion with him all the days of our lives. We see pictures of this friendship between humanity and God all through the Bible: in Adam walking with God in the garden in the cool of the evening; in Abraham's long pleading with God before Sodom; in Moses' long conversations with the Lord about the people of Israel; in Hannah pouring out her heart before the Lord at Shiloh; and here, in the stories of the beginning and end of Samuel's life.

A long friendship with God will have its seasons. But for the person called to lead, one of the most important times to pray and reflect is the moment of crisis and challenge, for the organization we lead and for ourselves. It is in the place of prayer that we find wisdom in complexity, peace in turmoil, guidance when we are lost and strength when we are empty. In order to be able to pray in that moment of crisis, the Christian leader needs to invest in this profound friendship with God through daily times of prayer, through learning its gentle disciplines and habits and through conversation with trusted friends. We need to learn to listen for God's voice as well as to speak with him.

Many years ago I experienced such a moment of stress. I felt called to leave the parish where I had been vicar for nine years. After months of waiting, I believed I had discovered the right role and place. I attended for interview. The following day I received a phone call to say that it would be a further week before there was a clear outcome from the process. I would be offered the post only if another candidate declined it. A week is not very long most of the time but those seven days stretched out ahead of me and seemed interminable. I phoned a friend and explained how I was feeling. She listened and, of course, advised me to pray and said she would pray for me. This helped. But then she said something which has stayed in my mind ever since: 'I don't know how people without faith manage in these situations without prayer.' If we are Christians and called to lead we have access to the richest resource and stream of support in the universe. This friendship is not available only to clergy: God makes friends with many different people – with politicians and business leaders, with chefs and entrepreneurs. This friendship is not available only to people of a certain age. God is in dialogue with Samuel as a child and as an old man. God's wisdom, guidance, strength and compassion are there for leaders in every situation at every stage of life if we will come to the place of prayer and listen.

Responding to change

At the beginning of this life crisis, Samuel's life has been in a settled, stable pattern for many years.

> Samuel went on a circuit year by year to Bethel, Gilgal and Mizpah; and he judged Israel in all those places. Then he would come back to Ramah for his home was there. (7.16–17)

The primary theme of the chapter is how a leader responds to change and, in particular, change which involves our own role. Sometimes we face this particular challenge near the beginning of a period of service, sometimes we face it near the end, as Samuel does here. It is seldom easy.

Samuel has lived much of his life in a settled pattern of leadership. His calling was to judge Israel: to offer leadership to the sometimes unruly confederation of tribes which made up the nation. Leadership for Samuel meant protecting the nation against its external enemies to bring peace and internally ordering its life to bring justice. He was singled out at birth and called to speak God's word as a child. He came into leadership of Israel after a great crisis and a victory over the Philistines. After this crisis his leadership settles into an annual pattern: a diligent circuit of the nation.

Samuel's faithful leadership year by year was a source of stability and the foundation of peace and justice in the land. But two different waves of change were growing and building. In this chapter we see them break over his head.

The first set of changes are internal. Samuel himself is growing older. What has been cannot continue for ever. The nation needs to take stock. Samuel made his own sons judges after him but they did not follow in his ways: they took bribes and perverted justice. The nation remembered what happened in the time of Eli, Samuel's immediate predecessor, when Samuel was a boy. Eli's sons were scoundrels. They grew fat on the offerings of the people and had to be removed from office under judgement. Succession planning is needed for the nation as Samuel grows older and is needed in every organization as leaders themselves change. Even so it cannot have been easy for Samuel (and it is not easy for anyone) to hear the words: 'You are old' (8.5).

But there were external changes taking place which Samuel can see only in part. There was an immense migration of peoples across the world. New communities were arriving in the territory occupied by Israel from the sea and creating new pressures and hunger for land. Samuel lived at the dawn of the iron age. New technology meant, as always, new weapons and different means of warfare. This new technology tilted the balance of power towards nations with dedicated warriors, a standing army, led by an experienced general, a king. Without clear leadership, the loose confederation of tribes was under threat from without but also from within. The final chapters of the Book of Judges make it clear that when there was no king in Israel 'all the people did what was right in their own eyes' (21.25). Justice and peace were both under threat.

These internal and external changes combined to create a crisis of leadership. The people come to Samuel and demanded a king (8.9). Fundamental change in any organization and a shift in power is seldom welcome. Like Samuel, our first response is to take it personally.

> But the thing displeased Samuel was when they said, 'Give us a king to govern us.' (8.10)

The people are offering Samuel a very different vision of his own future. We might assume that he expected life would carry on much as it had through the years and that Samuel's own sons would assume the mantle of his ministry in time. Now he is being told he must devote his remaining years to being the midwife of change. The present system cannot be abandoned, of course. The annual circuit will continue. But something new has to grow within and alongside the old. Samuel has a second vocation alongside the first. He must establish the monarchy, the kingship; a calling that will take the rest of his days.

1 Samuel 8 outlines the first steps in this process. Samuel takes his questions, his rejection, his sense of the complexity of the task to the Lord. God's response to this first set of questions is similar to Samuel's own. This is not uncommon:

'Listen to the voice of the people in all that they say to you for they have not rejected you but they have rejected me from being king over them'. (8:7)

Pause for a moment. We are eavesdropping here on a remarkable conversation in which God and Samuel are sharing together the pain of rejection and of change.

Samuel returns to the people and, in a memorable speech which still resonates today, the elderly prophet outlines the consequences and costs of kingship and the seriousness of the decision the nation is about to take:

'He will take your daughters to be perfumers and cooks and bakers. He will take the best of your fields and vineyards and give it to his officers and his courtiers. He will take your male and female slaves and the best of your cattle and donkeys and put them to his work. He will take one-tenth of your flocks and you shall be his slaves. And in that day you will cry out because of your king whom you have chosen for yourself; but the LORD will not answer you in that day.' (8.13–18)

The people listen but they are not persuaded. Again this is a moment of change. Samuel has occupied a position of respect for many years where 'the LORD was with him and let none of his words fall to the ground'. For the first time now he meets what every leader must meet in due course: the moment when those who have listened will no longer do so.

The people now return with their demands. There then is a wonderful phrase towards the end of the chapter which is worth pondering: 'When Samuel had heard all the words of the people, he repeated them in the ears of the LORD' (8.21). There is a slow and deliberate listening taking place here.

A Christian leader in any field will surely want to bring the cares and concerns and dilemmas of leadership to God in seasons of prayer at the beginning or at the end of each day. Those times and seasons will be a source of immense strength and wisdom. As leaders we will want to bring the hurtful or complex or challenging words people say to us and 'repeat them in the ears of the LORD' (8.21). In that simple act of rehearsal, repetition and reflection we will find the strength to listen and hear God's word to us in each situation.

Both the Lord and Samuel now agree to grant the people's request. The transition to kingship and a united monarchy will take many years. Samuel's first experiment, with Saul, will have to be abandoned. Only in David will kingship come to fulfil its potential and bring security and justice to the nation.

Drawing on friendship

Friendship with God is a most remarkable resource in exercising leadership in times of stability and also in times of change and transition. Samuel's friendship with God endured from childhood through to maturity and into the great crises of his later years when his routine was disrupted and his role transformed.

In times of stability, friendship with God offers strength and resources to endure, patience, love and companionship. In times of change, friendship with God provides vital space for reflection and to work through, in a loving dialogue, the most difficult issues of leadership and change.

Sooner or later in the life of any organization or community there is a cry for change. This happens in business, in churches, in schools and in families. When this cry for change happens near the beginning of a leader's tenure, it is challenging but seldom threatening. However, where the need for change becomes clear in a stable situation, where a person has been leading for many years, it will often be heard in a personal way: as criticism of the way things have been; as personal rejection. Sometimes change in organizations is resisted by those who lead because as leaders, we cannot move past this sense of rejection and personal critique.

Samuel offers us a model here. He takes his sense of hurt and rejection into his dialogue with God, into conversation. People might have that conversation in many different ways according to how they process difficult things. Some people are helped in that dialogue with God and others by journalling. Writing down what has happened and how we feel about it can be a way of untangling a ream of complex events and emotions, separating them out and exploring them. Others are helped by times of quiet and stillness as part of the day or as a special retreat. Still others will be helped by confidential conversations with a counsellor or spiritual accompanier. Again, the knots of difficult emotion can be faced and explored in a safe place before we determine the right way to respond. My own experience has been that all three of these ways are helpful. In times of transition and change, I need to pay more attention, not less, to what is happening within and rediscovering and drawing on friendship with God.

One of the things which happens through all of this process and reflection is that our first, sharp feelings of rejection soften. We begin to catch the perspective of those who have asked for change. We begin to realize that, very often, there have been internal and external shifts which do require a different response. We see past the temptation either to believe we have failed or to project blame, unfairly, onto others, both of which lead to despair. As that happens, we are then in the place where we can think through the possibility of change – including change in our own conduct and role and responsibilities.

Tending through change

Leaders in all kinds of organizations not only have to hear the call to change, but also to reflect on our emotional responses and to respond. We often have to communicate the need for organizational change to others and help them respond creatively to that challenge. In the story of Samuel, leaders often find themselves in the role of the elders of Israel, seeking a different way.

A high proportion of attempts to change organizations, charities and companies fail. There are many reasons for this but the story of Samuel's friendship with God has something to teach us here as well. Those you work with need particular care and friendship during seasons of change. People need more than clear vision and to understand the rationale for a particular change. They also need time to untangle their emotional responses to a particular plan and set of proposals and time to step back from their own role and see the bigger picture. Rational objections to what is being proposed need to be articulated and heard (as in Samuel's speech to the elders). The risks of the new way need to be assessed carefully. Not every pet scheme or idea is a good one.

A long friendship

Michael Ramsey was Archbishop of Canterbury through the turbulent period of the 1960s. In one of his most lasting books, *The Christian Priest Today*, Ramsey reflects that the role of the priest is to be a person of prayer: 'to be with God with the people on our heart'. This is a beautiful description of what it means to be a priest. However, I believe it captures something of the essence of what it means to exercise any sort of leadership in communities as a Christian disciple. We are caught up in a continuous dialogue with God on behalf of those we are called to serve, as was Samuel: being with God with the people on our hearts.

My favourite passage in Owen Chadwick's great biography of Ramsey comes at the very end of the book. Michael Ramsey had by then lived fourteen years in retirement (one of the greatest challenges of leadership of any kind as Samuel's story shows). Chadwick writes this:

> A young Muslim from Bangladesh, who kept the post office across the road where he used to buy stamps, came to visit him and asked how long he had been ordained. He said: 'Nearly sixty years.' The young man said: 'That's a very long friendship'; and Ramsey repeated the phrase more than once, savouring its memory and smiling.[1]

For Michael, for Samuel, for you and for me, the invitation to lead is an invitation to a very long friendship, to a dialogue which will continue for the whole of our lives.

---

1 Owen Chadwick, *Michael Ramsey: A Life*, Oxford: Oxford University Press, 1990, p. 398.

10

Vision

Numbers 13 and 14

Lord, help us to see

Enable with perpetual light
The dullness of our blinded sight.

Come Holy Ghost our souls inspire
(*veni creator spiritus*, trans. Bishop John Cosin)

These words form part of the great hymn to the Holy Spirit, sung at every service of ordination as men and woman are called and ordained to share in the leadership of God's people, the Church. They are a prayer for clear sight, for vision, as an essential part of that gift of leadership.

Sometimes vision emerges from the most unlikely places. Sometimes it will come from the youngest members of a community. St Benedict writes that when the community are summoned for counsel '. . . it is often to the younger that the Lord reveals what is best'. Sometimes vision will come from the oldest (and outwardly most conservative) members of the community.

Recently I visited one of the oldest churches in the Diocese of Sheffield, in a rural community. My reason for being there was to dedicate new building works. There is a new heating system, a new kitchen and space for children, a new organ, more flexible seating in the north aisle and a church extension to make room for a toilet. I always enjoy the blessing of a new water closet.

It's a great re-ordering. But what inspired me most was the vision that shaped it. Eight years ago, Mr Charles Round, a member of the church then in his eighties and a member of the choir, wrote this to the Rector. His letter followed the theft of lead from the roof of the organ loft which led in turn to damage to the organ, then one of the glories of this parish church.

The lead theft and the unfortunate resulting water damage to the organ may be a blessing in disguise which opens the door to a better use of the considerable space which the present pipe organ occupies. May I put the following ideas for your consideration? Instead of repairing the organ, clear out the organ loft and install a new electronic organ. The created area would provide a versatile and much needed space for our growing Sunday School . . . I feel it is time for objective, unemotional and realistic forward planning in order to assure the future continuous growth of our congregation and its influence in this parish.

When I visited the church, I saw a wonderful new facility, filled with young children and a church ready to welcome the next generation. It took eight years of patient work for Charles' vision to be fulfilled. But seeing clearly and naming that vision was an act of great courage.

Keeping the vision

Our final reflection on leadership is on this theme of vision, faithfulness to that vision and the courage required for that faithfulness. When vision fails, leaders in any walk of life cannot lead. The Book of Numbers tells the powerful story of twelve who were sent by Moses to spy out the land. It's a cautionary tale. Once again the Bible teaches positive lessons through negative experiences. God has brought the people of Israel out of slavery in Egypt. They have passed through the Red Sea. They have received the law. They have travelled through the desert, guided by the pillar of cloud and the pillar of fire and sustained by daily bread from heaven. Now they stand on the threshold of the Promised Land.

Moses chooses twelve, one from each tribe, to be the first to enter. Their task is clear. They are to see. We are told specifically and twice that every one of the twelve sent is to be a leader among the people (13.1, 3). The leaders are sent to catch the vision of a land flowing with milk and honey. They are to witness the goodness and fruitfulness of the Promised Land. They are to come back and inspire the whole people of Israel. The land is good. God is leading us on. It is worth persevering. There is an immeasurably better future than slavery in Egypt. There is an infinitely richer life than wandering through the wilderness. Keep going. Press forward.

But that is not what happens. These twelve, 'every one a leader', of the people lose their vision. They spend 40 days spying out the land. They return and speak to the people. There is indeed a rich land ahead, flowing with milk and honey. See, the fruit is good. They return carrying a branch with a single cluster of grapes which takes two men to lift. But they return carrying something else as well. Fear has gripped them. Their hearts are poisoned with despair.

Listen to what they say. They say that the inhabitants of the land are giants, that their cities are large and strong, that there are too many obstacles in the way. This is the most telling phrase. 'To ourselves we seemed like grasshoppers and so we seemed to them'. (13.33) Fear has corroded their perspective and their very identity.

Only two, Caleb and Joshua, sing a different song. They plead with the people to hold onto hope and pursue a better future. This people have seen God do so much. This is the generation which saw the plagues in Egypt, the Passover, the Red Sea. They have seen water flow from rock. But now they are gripped by fear. Rumour and terror and despair are infectious and spread quickly from the ten returning leaders to the rest of the people. Their courage and appetite for change ebbs away like the morning mist. The whole community stalls.

The failure is a failure of leadership and vision. Disaster is to follow. The people prefer, they say, two alternative visions of their future. One is a return to the comforts and challenges of slavery in Egypt. They are turning away from the possibility of realizing their own destiny and prefer an arduous journey back. What was in reality a life of back-breaking labour where their male children were thrown into the Nile, has become almost a picture of paradise compared to moving forward.

The second alternative is an endless wandering in the desert. The Israelites cry out to die in the desert. They have become settled in what was always meant to be an interim existence. Their hope and ambition have died and now they plead to die in this place. The present reality, a parched desert, becomes more attractive than the future hope.

God in his mercy grants their request. This is a sombre moment of judgement. The moment of opportunity when new vision can be realized has passed now. The Israelites saw God bring ten plagues on the Egyptians. Now they themselves have tested God in the wilderness ten times (14.22). For 40 more long years they will wander aimlessly in the wilderness, a people going round in circles, until a whole generation have died. Only Caleb and Joshua, the leaders and the keepers of the vision, will survive to lead the people into Canaan. Moses himself will come only to the threshold of what is promised. Why? Because the vision of the leaders of God's people failed.

Developing the vision

Whatever the leadership you exercise – in a school, a local authority, a church or a business – what is shaping your vision and keeping that vision alive?

You might want to draw a simple picture on a large piece of paper. Imagine the community or organization you lead and let it serve as the Israelites camped in the desert. Look to the left of the camp, back down the road. Where has this business or organization come from? What is its story and journey? What are the milestones on the way?

Now look to the right of the camp, further ahead. What is the vision of the future, the Promised Land, the substance of your hope for this organization and community?

For the Israelites, the content of the vision was wide and deep: freedom from slavery, peace and security, the ability to flourish in the land promised to their forefathers, the ability to worship the God who has called them and be a blessing to all the peoples of the earth.

The vision for your own organization or community will be different. It may be to make the city you live in one of the fairest in Britain. It may be to grow the quality of education for every child in your school. It may be to improve the quality of safeguarding in your local authority so that every child and adult can flourish. It may be to eliminate corruption, or to increase the order book so that the people who work in your company have secure jobs and futures, or to grow a new congregation in your local church. It may be to reduce child poverty, to feed the hungry in your community, to start a new group for young people or to radically reduce the child death rate from lack of clean drinking water.

All of these visions, for a Christian, will flow from and connect with our faith and with the vision for human flourishing which emerges from the scriptures and from the person and work of Jesus Christ. But the general vision of the scriptures becomes concrete and specific as we distil it and pray through it and consider our own reality and calling. However, an essential part of being a Christian leader is a holy discontent with the way the world is now and a longing for it to be better in specific and real ways which make a difference in people's lives and then to dedicate yourself, with others, to making that vision a reality. All too often, leaders who are Christians neglect to nurture a fresh vision of what is possible within our own situation and our leadership is less than it could be.

Once you have sketched the vision of the Promised Land, flowing with milk and honey, in your picture, draw one more thing. Draw the Amalekites, the Hittites, the Jebusites and the Canaanites in the land of your vision. Sketch in the giants, which make you look and feel like a grasshopper. Name them.

It is important to realize that any vision for human flourishing or organization which is worthy of the name 'vision' will be difficult. The more worthwhile it seems, the more difficulties there will be. The twelve leaders who are sent to explore the Promised Land are sent partly for this reason. So take some time to name your Amalekites. There may be challenges of resources; of commitment; of personnel. There may be market forces and pressures. There may be deep-seated attitudes in the community you serve. There may be particular individuals who stand in the way: a real opposition to be overcome. There may be a spiritual dynamic to the situation, which is unseen.

Take some moments then to see the whole picture: the camp in the wilderness, the journey you have made so far, the vision of the Promised Land and the obstacles which stand in the way. What kind of report are you bringing back from your expedition to scout out the land? Are you with Caleb and Joshua or with the ten? Are you coming back to the camp to rekindle faith and lead your organization or your family to a better future? Or are you returning to spread despair and to counsel your community to be content with slavery and satisfied with the desert?

Clarity of vision

For some who do this exercise, the real problem will be that you have lost sight of the Promised Land altogether: your leadership is no longer shaped and motivated by a vision of a different future. Our sight has become dulled and our imagination corroded by the constant demands of the present. Perhaps this is exactly where Moses is in this narrative of rebellion. He is exhausted by the demands of leading the exodus from Egypt and the journey through the wilderness.

We cannot lead unless we have a clear vision of where we are going. If that is your own situation then take time to see clearly. Begin with prayer for clarity of sight. You might want to use the prayer to the Holy Spirit at the beginning of the chapter:

Enable with perpetual light the dullness of our blinded sight.

You might want to borrow the prayer of blind Bartimaeus to Jesus in Mark 10.51:

'My teacher, let me see again.'

You may want to ponder the invitation of the risen Christ in Revelation 3.18 to the Church in Laodicaea:

'I counsel you to buy from me . . . salve to anoint your eyes so that you may see.'

Follow on from this prayer with a second step: remind yourself of the vision for human life and for human flourishing and for the world which is present in the Scriptures and in the life, ministry, death and resurrection of Jesus Christ. This is a vision which should be continually nurtured in every Christian through prayer and Bible reading and most of all through engaging in the worship of the Church, and especially in the Eucharist. The worship of the Church is where our vision of God is continually stretched and expanded together with our vision of God's intentions for the world. In this nurturing of vision we will pay particular attention to the dignity and worth of every human person and to God's call to justice and peace and to the care of the earth.

This prayer and immersion in a fresh vision of God and for the world is not the work of moments: it may take some weeks or months or even years. But when your eyes are open again to

God's nature and God's purpose for the world, return again to the community or organization or business that you lead and begin to describe, first to yourself and then to others, your vision for change and development in that context.

'Where there is no vision, the people perish,' says the old translation of Proverbs 29.18. The verse is an exact description of what happens in Numbers and in any context where leaders lack a vision for a different future. An essential part of exercising leadership in any organization is to invest time in first developing and then communicating that vision for a creative future.

Interpreting the vision

But there is one more step to this journey. All twelve who are sent out see the same Promised Land. All twelve taste of its fruit. All twelve see the Amalekites, the Hittites, the Jebusites and the Canaanites.

Ten return crippled by fear and despair and spread that despair to others. Two return full of hope and ready to lead the people up to inherit what God has promised to them. What is it that makes the difference?

Caleb and Joshua maintain their vision of God and what God is able to do even in the midst of an assessment of the challenges ahead:

> 'If the LORD is pleased with us, he will bring us into this land and give it to us, a land that flows with milk and honey. Only do not fear the people of the land for they are no more than bread for us; their protection is removed from them and the LORD is with us; do not fear them.' (14.8–9)

At the beginning of this exploration of leadership according to the Scriptures, I argued that one of the central insights into leadership in the Christian tradition is that the exercise of leadership in communities is extremely difficult. Our final story in Numbers underlines the challenges faced by Moses.

However, there is a further step in this understanding of leadership as difficult. It is the joyful acceptance of impossibly difficult challenges which we find all the way through scripture.

I love the Mission Impossible films and particularly the part at the beginning of each story where Tom Cruise and his team receive their impossible challenge: 'Your mission, if you choose to accept it . . .' There follows the disclaimer that failure will result in being disavowed and the inevitable: 'this tape will self-destruct in five seconds'.

For several years I used the Mission Impossible theme as my mobile phone ringtone. It caused some strange looks on trains. I did so because of a particular commission I was given to set up and lead Fresh Expressions, which had the task of enabling fresh expressions of church to flourish across the whole of the Church of England and the Methodist Church, initially in a five-year timeframe.

Humanly speaking, this was an impossible mission. There were formidable obstacles. There were Amalekites on every side. But I came to discover that there was real grace and joy in the impossibility of the task. Of course it was impossible, humanly speaking. But that very impossibility created a freedom to take risks, to step out in faith, to be bold and to see what God would do. Of course it was impossible, and I had no idea how to set out that task. But that very impossibility created a desire to pray, to seek help from others wherever I could, to work collaboratively and not alone and to find great joy in the task.

I came to realize that, in reality, every other leadership role I had ever been asked to fulfil was also impossible, from a human perspective, and only realizable through grace. And that, I have found, is a very good place to live as a leader: constantly to nourish impossible visions of God's grace and seek to see them fulfilled and realized, not in my own strength but through God at work in many different ways and people.

God calls his people, the Church, to many different forms of leadership in many different places and organizations. The Holy Spirit is given so that old people might dream dreams and young people might see visions. God is still calling people in many different ways to impossible missions and then going ahead of them and enabling great change.

May God bless you in the leadership you offer all the days of your life and may you abide in his love for ever.

O LORD, my heart is not lifted up,
My eyes are not raised too high,
I do not occupy myself with things too great and too marvellous for me.
But I have calmed and quieted my soul,
Like a weaned child with its mother;
My soul is like the weaned child that is with me.

O Israel, hope in the LORD,
From this time on and for evermore. (Psalm 131)